Listen for It

Focus The alphabet has 26 letters. Some letters are **consonants**. Some letters are **vowels**.
The letters **a, e, i, o,** and **u** are vowels.

Name each letter. Circle the vowels.

a b c d e f g

h i j k l m n

o p q r s t u

v w x y z

There are **five vowels** in the alphabet.
Write the vowels on the lines.

1. _____   2. _____   3. _____   4. _____   5. _____

Dictation

Write your name. Circle the vowels.

_____

Listen for It

Day 2 | Week 1

Focus Each consonant has its own special sound.

Say the letter-sound.
Draw a line to the picture that begins with that letter-sound.

b

c

d

f

g

h

j

Dictation ··

Circle the vowels.

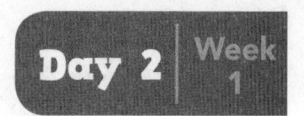

I can go.

Listen for It

Day 3 | Week 1

Focus Each consonant has its own special sound.

Say the letter-sound.
Draw a line to the picture that begins with that letter-sound.

k

l

m

n

p

q

r

s

Dictation

Circle the vowels.

Run fast, _____.
(name)

Listen and Write It

Day 4 | Week 1

> **Focus** Each consonant has its own special sound.

Say the letter-sound.
Draw a line to the picture that begins with that letter-sound.

t

v

w

x

y

z

Finish the alphabet. Write the missing letters. Then name each letter.

a b ___ d ___ ___ g h ___ j ___ ___ m ___

o p ___ ___ ___ t ___ ___ w x ___ ___

Dictation

Circle the vowels.

I can go fast.

Listen for It

Day 5 | Week 1

Focus: The letters **a**, **e**, **i**, **o**, and **u** are vowels. Each vowel has a **short** and a **long** sound. The **long** sound says its name.

short a	short e	short i	short o	short u
long a	long e	long i	long o	long u

Say the picture name. Circle the picture if you hear the **long** vowel sound.

1. a
2. e
3. i
4. o
5. u

© Evan-Moor Corp. • EMC 6772 • Daily Phonics

Listen for It

Day 1 | Week 2

Focus: Consonants can appear at the beginning or the end of a word.

| b | **b**ed | tu**b** |

| f | **f**an | lea**f** |

Say the sound of the letter. Then say the picture name.
Fill in the circle to show if you hear the letter-sound **first** or **last**.

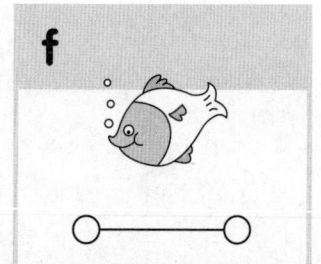

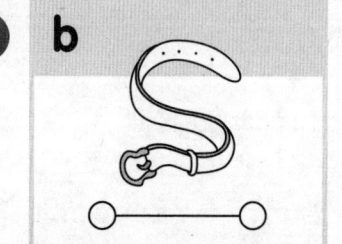

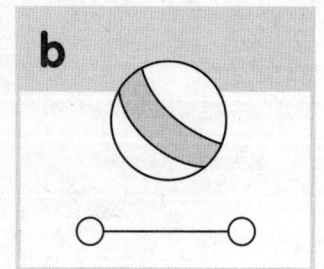

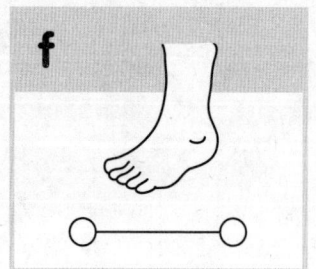

1. b
2. f
3. b
4. f
5. b
6. f
7. b
8. f
9. b

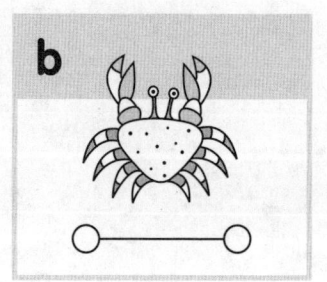

Dictation

1. ____us
2. tu____
3. ____at
4. el____

Listen for It

Day 2 | Week 2

Focus: Consonants can appear at the beginning or the end of a word.

| m | moon | worm | | s | sock | bus |

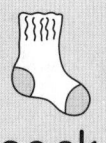

Say the sound of the letter. Then say the picture name.
Fill in the circle to show if you hear the letter-sound **first** or **last**.

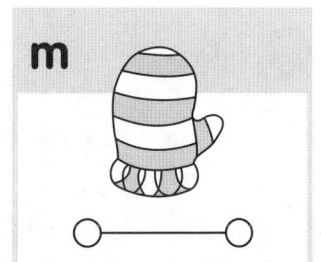

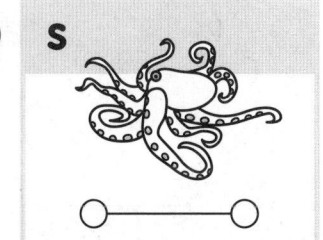

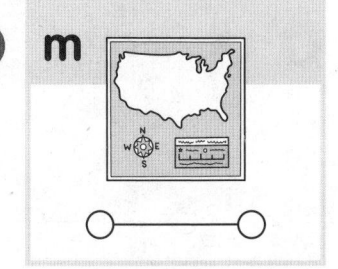

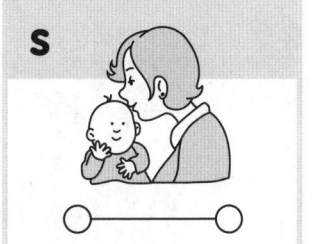

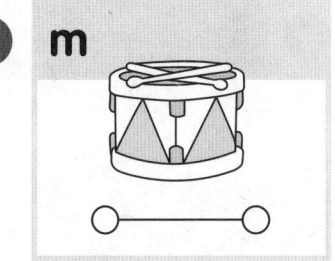

1. s (sailboat)
2. m (mitten)
3. s (octopus)
4. m (map)
5. s (mother with baby)
6. m (drum)
7. s (seal)
8. m (clam)
9. s (walnut)

Dictation

1. ___op   2. gu___   3. ___at   4. ga___

Listen for It

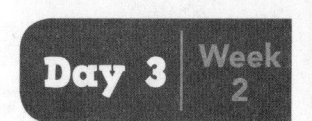

Day 3 | Week 2

Focus Consonants can appear at the beginning or the end of a word.

| k | 🔑 key | 🍴 forK | | p | 🍳 pan | 📮 stamP |

Say the sound of the letter. Then say the picture name.
Fill in the circle to show if you hear the letter-sound **first** or **last**.

1. k
2. p
3. k
4. p
5. p
6. k
7. p
8. k
9. p

Dictation ···

1. ___it   2. des___   3. ___en   4. la___

8 Daily Phonics • EMC 6772 • © Evan-Moor Corp.

Write It

Day 4 | Week 2

Letter Box
b f m s k p

Say the picture name.
Write the letter that stands for the **first** letter-sound you hear.

1. ___us	2. ___oon	3. ___ite
4. ___ox	5. ___un	6. ___ing
7. ___ig	8. ___ag	9. ___an
10. ___an	11. ___ock	12. ___an

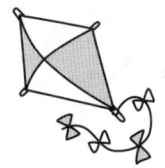

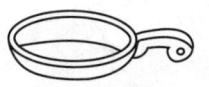

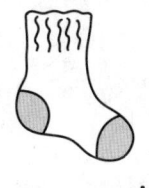

Dictation

1. ___it   2. ___an   3. ___ap   4. ___ed

Write It

Day 5 | Week 2

Letter Box

b f m s k p

Say the picture name.
Write the letter that stands for the **last** letter-sound you hear.

1. tu____
2. roo____
3. nut____
4. ja____
5. des____
6. ma____
7. lea____
8. cra____
9. gu____
10. mo____
11. wor____
12. for____

Dictation

1. ha____
2. bu____
3. sa____
4. ru____

Listen for It

Day 1 | Week 3

Focus: Consonants can appear at the beginning or the end of a word.

| d | dollar | bed | | n | nest | fan |

Say the sound of the letter. Then say the picture name.
Fill in the circle to show if you hear the letter-sound **first** or **last**.

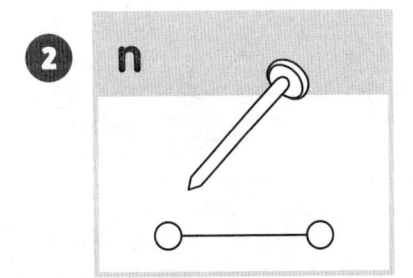

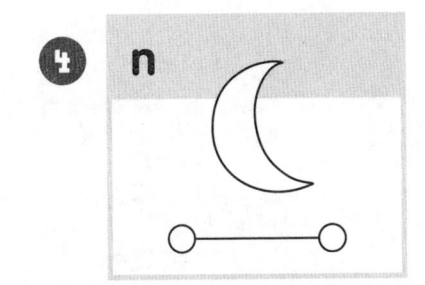

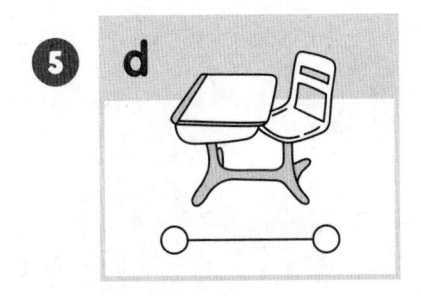

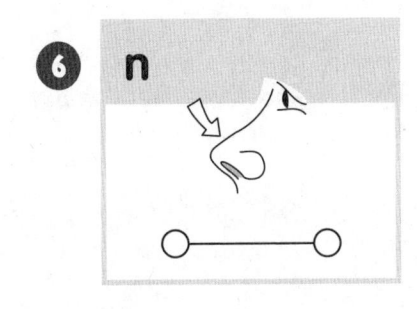

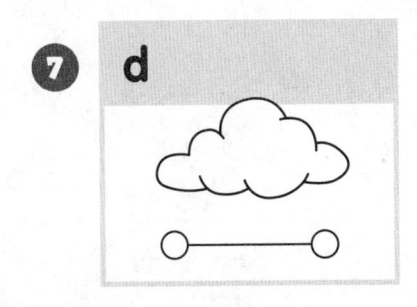

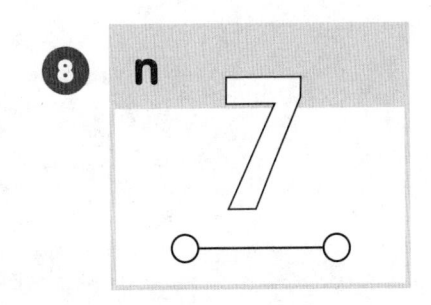

1. d (duck)
2. n (nail)
3. d (bread)
4. n (moon)
5. d (desk)
6. n (nose)
7. d (cloud)
8. n (7)
9. d (doll)

Dictation

1. ___e___   2. ___o___   3. ___a___

Listen for It

Day 2 | Week 3

Focus: Consonants can appear at the beginning or the end of a word.

r | rake | star

g | gate | frog

Say the sound of the letter. Then say the picture name.
Fill in the circle to show if you hear the letter-sound **first** or **last**.

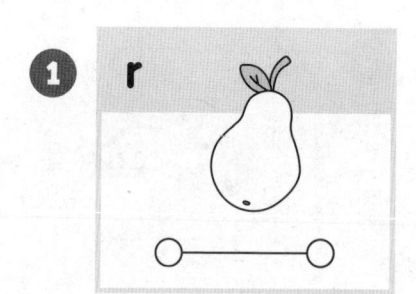

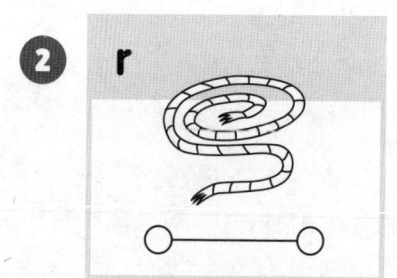

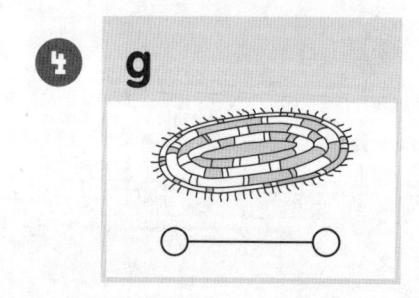

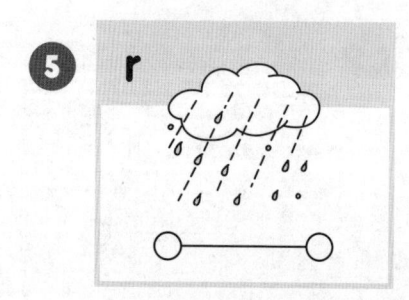

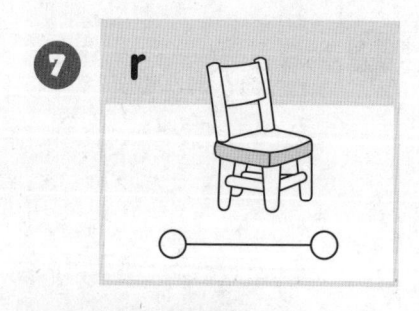

1. r
2. r
3. g
4. g
5. r
6. g
7. r
8. g
9. g

Dictation

1. ___a___   2. ___o___   3. ___a___

Listen for It

Day 3 | Week 3

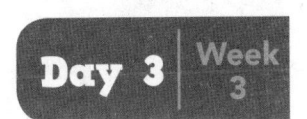

Focus: Consonants can appear at the beginning or the end of a word.

| t | 10 ten | jet | | l | leaf | seal |

Say the sound of the letter. Then say the picture name.
Fill in the circle to show if you hear the letter-sound **first** or **last**.

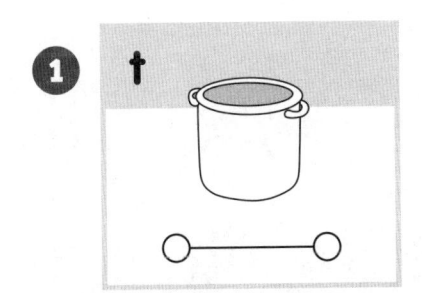

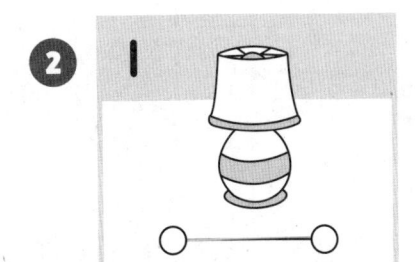

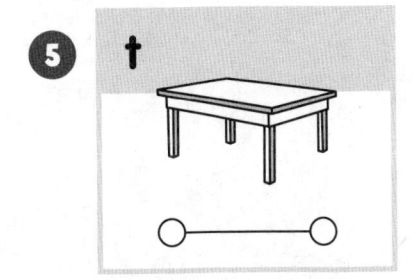

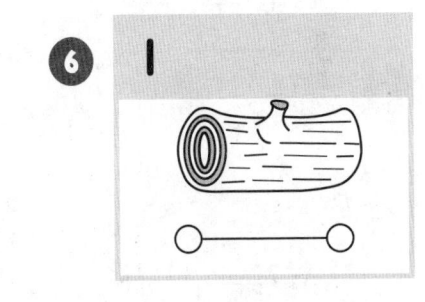

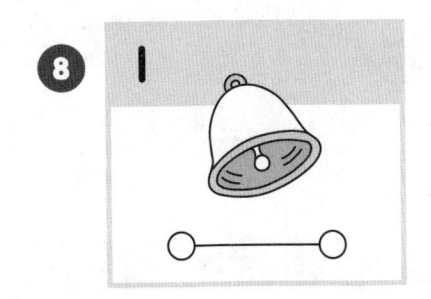

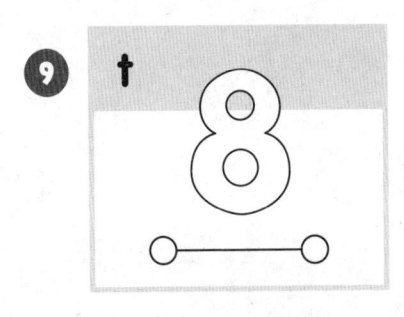

1. t — (pot)
2. l — (lamp)
3. l — (owl)
4. l — (pail)
5. t — (table)
6. l — (log)
7. l — (lock)
8. l — (bell)
9. t — (8)

Dictation

1. ___a___   2. ___e___   3. ___a___

13

Write It

Day 4 | Week 3

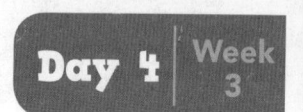

Letter Box

d n n r g t l

Say the picture name.
Write the letter that stands for the **first** letter-sound you hear.

1. ___oll
2. ___ift
3. ___ose
4. ___est
5. ___en
6. ___og
7. ___obot
8. ___ion
9. ___et
10. ___ooth
11. ___ug
12. ___irl

Dictation ··

1. ___ed   2. ___ed   3. ___ip   4. ___ip

14   Daily Phonics • EMC 6772 • © Evan-Moor Corp.

Write It

Day 5 | Week 3

Letter Box
d n r g t l

Say the picture name.
Write the letter that stands for the **last** letter-sound you hear.

1. ca____
2. pi____
3. be____
4. fa____
5. bir____
6. ten____
7. sta____
8. ru____
9. han____
10. came____
11. dee____
12. fla____

Dictation

1. do____   2. ro____   3. go____   4. ru____

Listen for It

Day 1 | Week 4

Focus The letter **a** is a vowel. It has the /ă/ sound you hear in **cat**. This is called the **short a** sound.

| short **a** |  | c**a**t |

Say the picture name.
Fill in the circle next to **yes** if you hear the sound of **short a**.
Fill in the circle next to **no** if you do not hear the sound of **short a**.

1  ○ yes ○ no

2  ○ yes ○ no

3  ○ yes ○ no

4  ○ yes ○ no

5  ○ yes ○ no

6 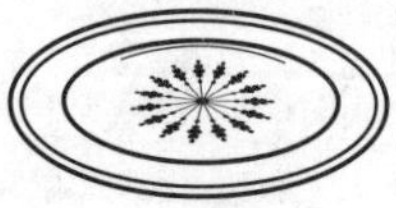 ○ yes ○ no

7  ○ yes ○ no

8 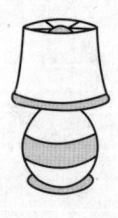 ○ yes ○ no

9  ○ yes ○ no

Dictation

1. ____ ____ ____   2. ____ ____ ____   3. ____ ____ ____

Listen for It

Day 2 | Week 4

Focus: The letter **i** is a vowel. It has the /ĭ/ sound you hear in **lips**. This is called the **short i** sound.

| short i | | lips |

Say the picture name.
Fill in the circle next to **yes** if you hear the sound of **short i**.
Fill in the circle next to **no** if you do not.

1. ○ yes ○ no

2. ○ yes ○ no

3. ○ yes ○ no

4. ○ yes ○ no

5. ○ yes ○ no

6. ○ yes ○ no

7. ○ yes ○ no

8. ○ yes ○ no

9. ○ yes ○ no

Dictation

1. _____   2. _____   3. _____

Listen for It

Day 3 | Week 4

Focus Some words have a **short** vowel sound in the middle.

short **a**		short **i**	
cat		lips	

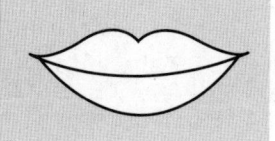

Say the picture name. Listen for the middle sound.
Fill in the circle next to the letter that stands for the vowel sound you hear.

1. ○ a   ○ i
2. ○ a   ○ i
3. ○ a   ○ i
4. ○ a   ○ i
5. ○ a   ○ i
6. ○ a   ○ i
7. ○ a   ○ i
8. ○ a   ○ i
9. ○ a   ○ i

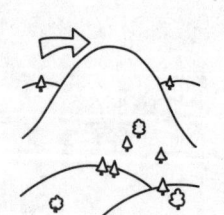

Dictation ....

_____ in a _____

Write It

Day 4 | Week 4

Letter Box

a   i

Say the picture name.
Write the letter that stands for the **short** vowel sound you hear.

1. 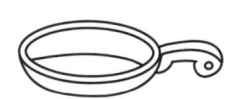 p __ n
2.  w __ g
3.  f __ n
4.  p __ n
5.  h __ m
6.  d __ g
7.  r __ t
8.  b __ b
9.  s __ t

Dictation

___ ___ ___ in a ___ ___ ___

© Evan-Moor Corp. • EMC 6772 • Daily Phonics

19

Read It

Day 5 | Week 4

Write the missing words. Then read the sentence.

1. sit   pig

   The _____ can _____.

2. wig   rat

   The _____ has a _____.

3. sun   big

   The _____ is _____.

4. bag   pig

   The _____ is in a _____.

Dictation

The _____ _____ _____.

Listen for It

Day 1 | **Week 5**

Focus: The letter **e** is a vowel. It has the /ĕ/ sound you hear in **jet**. This is called the **short e** sound.

| short **e** |  | **je**t |

Say the picture name.
Fill in the circle next to **yes** if you hear the sound of **short e**.
Fill in the circle next to **no** if you do not hear the sound of **short e**.

1. 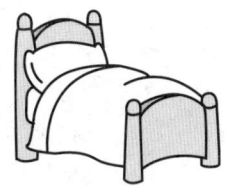 ○ yes ○ no
2.  ○ yes ○ no
3.  ○ yes ○ no
4.  ○ yes ○ no
5.  ○ yes ○ no
6. 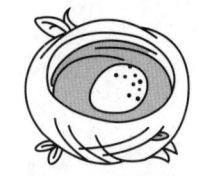 ○ yes ○ no
7. 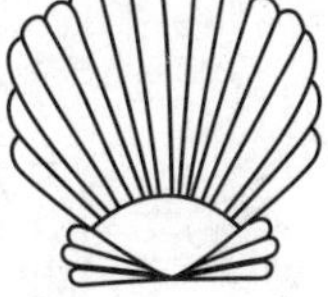 ○ yes ○ no
8.  ○ yes ○ no
9.  ○ yes ○ no

Dictation

1. _____ _____ _____   2. _____ _____ _____   3. _____ _____ _____

Listen for It

Day 2 | Week 5

Focus: The letter **o** is a vowel. It has the /ŏ/ sound you hear in **box**. This is called the **short o** sound.

| short **o** | | b**o**x |

Say the picture name.
Fill in the circle next to **yes** if you hear the sound of **short o**.
Fill in the circle next to **no** if you do not hear the sound of **short o**.

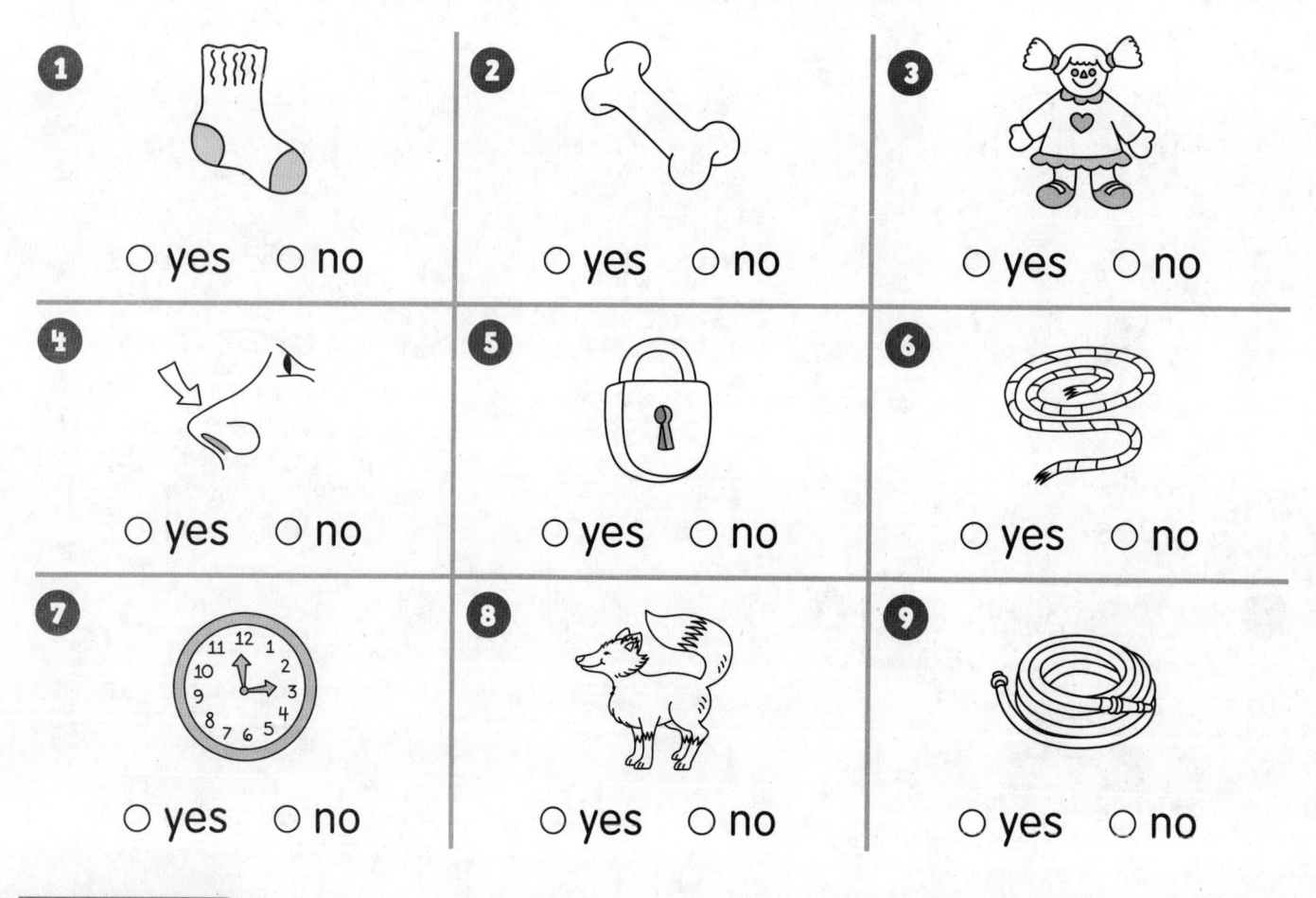

1. ○ yes ○ no
2. ○ yes ○ no
3. ○ yes ○ no
4. ○ yes ○ no
5. ○ yes ○ no
6. ○ yes ○ no
7. ○ yes ○ no
8. ○ yes ○ no
9. ○ yes ○ no

Dictation ....

1. ___ ___ ___   2. ___ ___ ___   3. ___ ___ ___

Listen for It

Day 3 | Week 5

Focus: The letter **u** is a vowel. It has the /ŭ/ sound you hear in **cup**. This is called the **short u** sound.

| short u | | cup |

Say the picture name.
Fill in the circle next to **yes** if you hear the sound of **short u**.
Fill in the circle next to **no** if you do <u>not</u> hear the sound of **short u**.

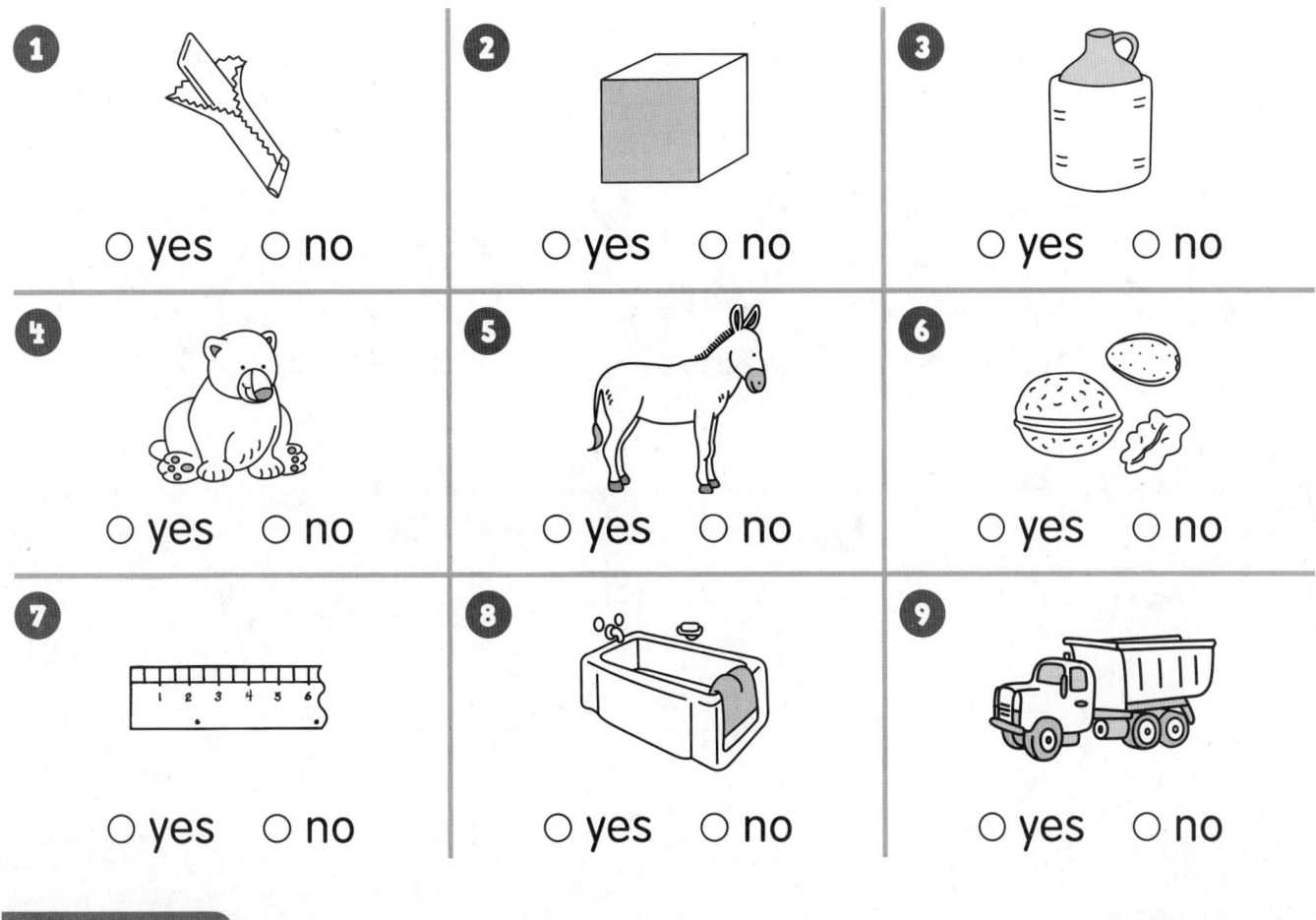

1. ○ yes ○ no

2. ○ yes ○ no

3. ○ yes ○ no

4. ○ yes ○ no

5. ○ yes ○ no

6. ○ yes ○ no

7. ○ yes ○ no

8. ○ yes ○ no

9. ○ yes ○ no

Dictation

1. _____   2. _____   3. _____

Write It

Day 4 | Week 5

Letter Box

e   o   u

Say the picture name.
Write the letter that stands for the **short** vowel sound you hear.

1. h___n
2. l___ck
3. b___s
4. p___p
5. m___p
6. t___nt
7. f___x
8. l___g
9. g___m

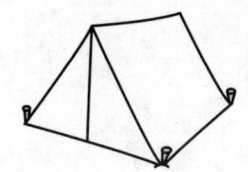

Dictation

a ___ ___ ___   ___ ___ ___

Read It

Day 5 | Week 5

Write the missing words. Then read the sentence.

1

nest   up

The _____ is _____.

2

doll   hug

I _____ my _____.

3

pup   wet

My _____ is _____.

4

pen   hen

The _____ is in the _____.

Dictation •••

The j___t went ___p.

Listen for It

Day 1 | Week 6

Focus: A vowel between two consonants has a **short** sound.

r-a-t
rat

b-e-d
bed

d-i-g
dig

l-o-g
log

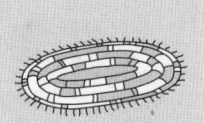

r-u-g
rug

Say the picture name. Listen to the vowel sound.
Write the letter that stands for that sound.

1.  n___t
2.  h___t
3. 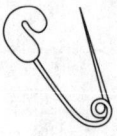 p___n
4.  h___g
5.  w___g
6.  c___n
7.  w___b
8.  c___b
9.  d___g

Dictation

1. ____ ____ ____   2. ____ ____ ____   3. ____ ____ ____

26   Daily Phonics • EMC 6772 • © Evan-Moor Corp.

Listen for It

Day 2 | Week 6

Focus: Words that have a **short** vowel sound between two consonants are called **CVC words**.

m–a–n
m**a**n

n–e–t
n**e**t

p–i–g
p**i**g

p–o–t
p**o**t

s–u–n
s**u**n

Say the picture name. Listen to the vowel sound.
Fill in the circle next to the correct word.

1.  ○ hen
   ○ hip

2.  ○ cut
   ○ cat

3.  ○ gum
   ○ get

4. 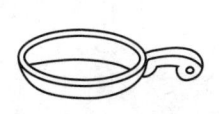 ○ pen
   ○ pan

5.  ○ dog
   ○ dig

6.  ○ bad
   ○ bed

7.  ○ cub
   ○ cab

8.  ○ bob
   ○ bib

9.  ○ leg
   ○ log

Dictation

1. _____ _____ _____   2. _____ _____ _____   3. _____ _____ _____

Write It

Day 3 | Week 6

Letter Box
a e i o u

Say the picture name.
Write the letter that stands for the vowel sound you hear.

1. f ___ n

2. m ___ p

3. g ___ m

4. s ___ x

5. t ___ b

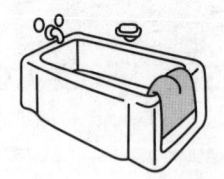

6. p ___ t

7. p ___ g

8. t ___ n

9. j ___ m

Dictation

1. ___ ___ ___   2. ___ ___ ___   3. ___ ___ ___

28 Daily Phonics • EMC 6772 • © Evan-Moor Corp.

Read It

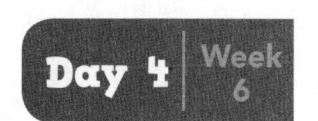

Day 4 | Week 6

Read the sentence. Fill in the circle beside the missing word. Then write the word on the line.

1 It is a _____. ○ hat   ○ hot

2 His _____ is a pet. ○ hit   ○ hen

3 The _____ is with its mom. ○ cub   ○ cab

4 Sit on the _____. ○ log   ○ leg

5 It is in the _____. ○ nut   ○ net

6 The pig dug in the _____. ○ mud   ○ mad

Dictation

a ___ ___ ___ in a ___ ___ ___

Read It

Day 5 | Week 6

Write the missing words. Then read the sentence.

1

mud   pig

See the _____ in the _____.

2

net   bug

See the _____ in the _____.

3

cat   hat

See the _____ in the _____.

4

pen   dog

See the _____ in the _____.

Dictation ···

_____ on a _____

Listen for It

Day 1 | Week 7

Focus: The vowels **a**, **e**, and **o** have a long sound. The **long** sound says the vowel's name.

long **a**	long **e**	long **o**
ape	h**e**	n**o**

Say the picture name.
Fill in the circle next to the **long** vowel sound you hear.

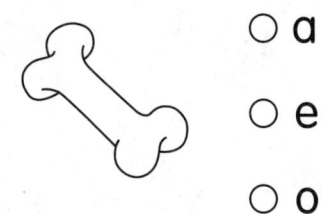

1. 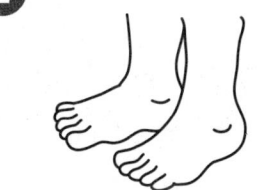 ○ a ○ e ○ o
2.  ○ a ○ e ○ o
3.  ○ a ○ e ○ o
4.  ○ a ○ e ○ o
5.  ○ a ○ e ○ o
6.  ○ a ○ e ○ o
7. ○ a ○ e ○ o
8.  ○ a ○ e ○ o
9.  ○ a ○ e ○ o

Dictation ....

1. _____ _____   2. _____ _____   3. _____ _____

© Evan-Moor Corp. • EMC 6772 • Daily Phonics

Listen for It

Day 2 | Week 7

Focus: The vowels **i** and **u** have a long sound.
The **long** vowel says the vowel's name.

long **i** b**i**ke

long **u** m**u**sic

Say the picture name.
Fill in the circle next to the **long** vowel sound you hear.

1. ○ i ○ u
2. ○ i ○ u
3. ○ i ○ u
4. ○ i ○ u
5. ○ i ○ u
6. ○ i ○ u
7. ○ i ○ u
8. ○ i ○ u
9. ○ i ○ u

Dictation

1. ___ ___ e   2. ___ ___ e   3. ___ ___ e

Write It

Day 3 | Week 7

Letter Box
a   e   i   o   u

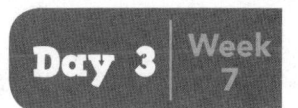

Say the picture name.
Write the letter that stands for the vowel sound you hear.

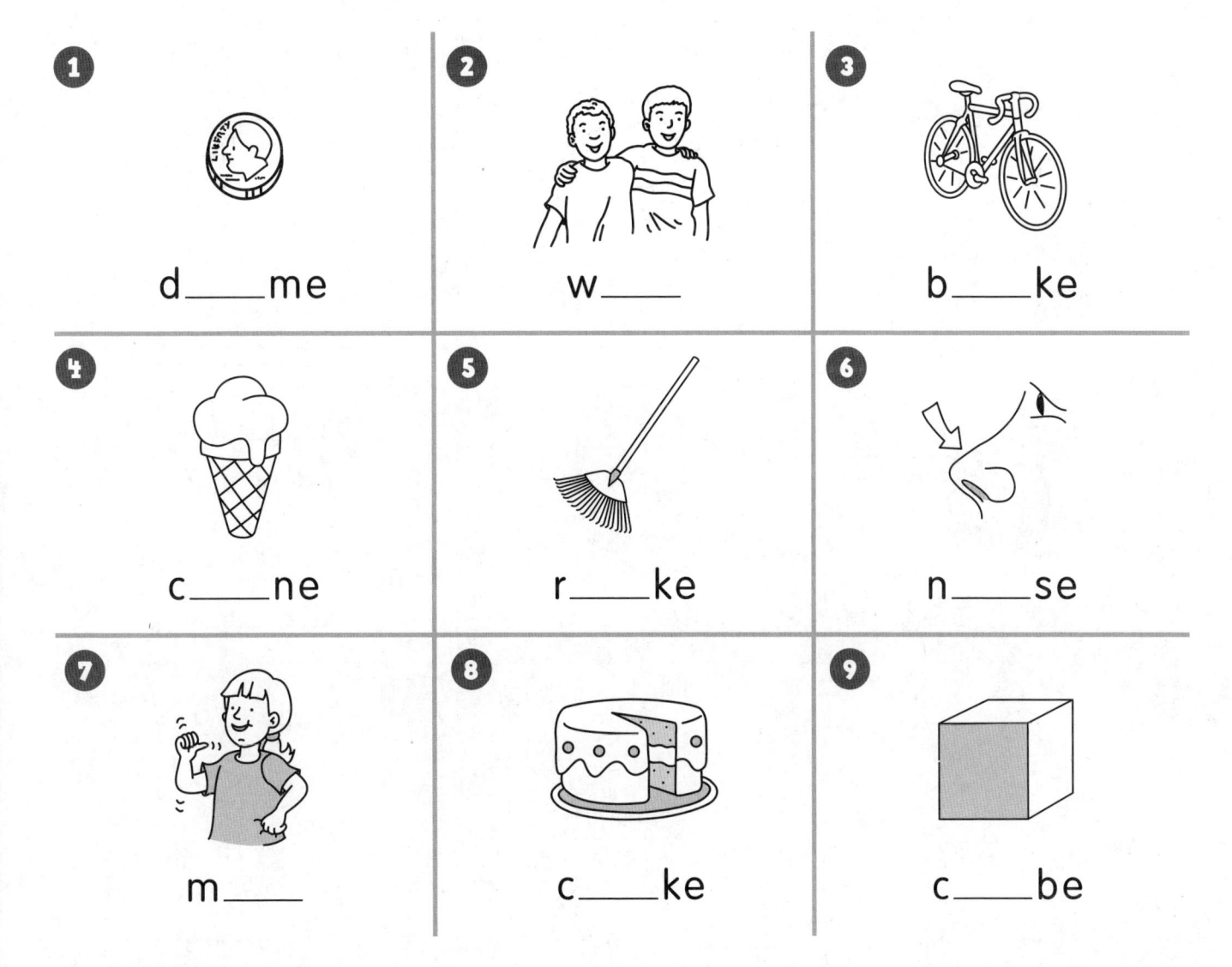

1. d___me
2. w___
3. b___ke
4. c___ne
5. r___ke
6. n___se
7. m___
8. c___ke
9. c___be

Dictation

___ ___ ___e the ___ ___ ___e

© Evan-Moor Corp. • EMC 6772 • Daily Phonics

33

Write It

Day 4 | Week 7

Letter Box
a   e   i   o   u

Say the picture name. Write the letter that stands for the vowel sound you hear. Read the word.

1. t___be
2. h___se
3. t___pe
4. c___pe
5. t___re
6. m___le
7. b___ne
8. f___ve
9. r___pe

Dictation

___ ___ ___e the ___ ___ ___e

Review It

Day 5 | Week 7

Say the picture name.
Circle the pictures that have a **long** vowel sound.
Underline the pictures that have a **short** vowel sound.

1. a
2. e
3. i
4. o
5. u

Dictation

___ ___ ___e the ___ ___e

Listen for It

Day 1 | Week 8

Focus: Add an **e** to a CVC word to make the vowel sound **long**. The final **e** in a CVCe word has no sound, but it tells you that the vowel sound in the middle is long.

cub + e = cube

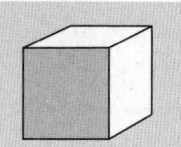

Write an **e** to make the vowel sound **long**. Then read the word.
Fill in the circle under the picture that matches the word.

1. man___

2. pin___

3. cap___

4. rob___

5. tap___

6. can___

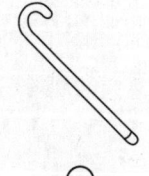

Dictation

1. ____ ____ ____   2. ____ ____ ____ ____

Write It

Day 2 | Week 8

Letter Box
a   e   i   o   u

Say the picture name. Write the letter that stands for the **long** vowel sound. Then write a final **e** at the end of the word.

1.  r___p___

2.  w___v___

3. 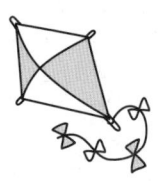 k___t___

4.  f___v___

5.  m___l___

6.  r___b___

7.  t___p___

8.  pl___n___

9.  fl___t___

Dictation

1. ____ ____ ____ ____   2. ____ ____ ____ ____

Write It

Day 3 | Week 8

Word Box

tire   wave   rake
mule   nine   hose

Say the picture name. Write the word on the lines.
Then circle the silent **e**.

1. ___ ___ ___ ___
2. ___ ___ ___ ___
3. ___ ___ ___ ___
4. ___ ___ ___ ___
5. ___ ___ ___ ___
6. ___ ___ ___ ___

Dictation ....

1. ___ ___ ___ ___   2. ___ ___ ___ ___

Write It

Day 4 | Week 8

Word Box

rake	bite	cute	lake
pole	cave	lime	bone
cube	mule	cone	time

Read each word. Listen to the **long** vowel sound.
Write the word in the correct box.

long a
_____
_____

long i
_____
_____

long o
_____
_____

long u
_____
_____

Dictation ....

1. ____ ____ ____   2. ____ ____ ____

Read It

Day 5 | Week 8

Write the missing words. Then read the sentence.

1

wet   hose

The _____ got her _____.

2

bike   rat

The _____ is on a _____.

3

big   cone

He has a _____ _____.

4

cake   pig

I see a _____ with a _____.

Dictation

1. ____ ____ ____ ____   2. ____ ____ ____ ____

Listen for It

Day 1 | Week 9

Focus: A syllable is a word part that has one vowel sound.

| **1** syllable |  mop | **2** syllables |  monkey |

Say the picture name. How many syllables do you hear?
Fill in the circle next to the correct number.

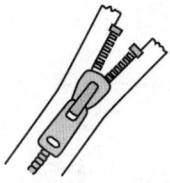

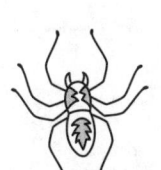

1  baby — ○ 1 ○ 2

2 bone — ○ 1 ○ 2

3 mitten — ○ 1 ○ 2

4 star — ○ 1 ○ 2

5 zipper — ○ 1 ○ 2

6 desk — ○ 1 ○ 2

7 flag — ○ 1 ○ 2

8 zebra — ○ 1 ○ 2

9 spider — ○ 1 ○ 2

Dictation

1. ___ ___ ___ ☐   2. ___ ___ ___ ☐

© Evan-Moor Corp. • EMC 6772 • Daily Phonics

Read It

Day 2 | Week 9

Focus: Many words are divided into syllables between two consonants. Each syllable has a vowel.

t e n | n i s   m a g | n e t

Draw a line to divide the word into syllables. Underline the vowel in each syllable.

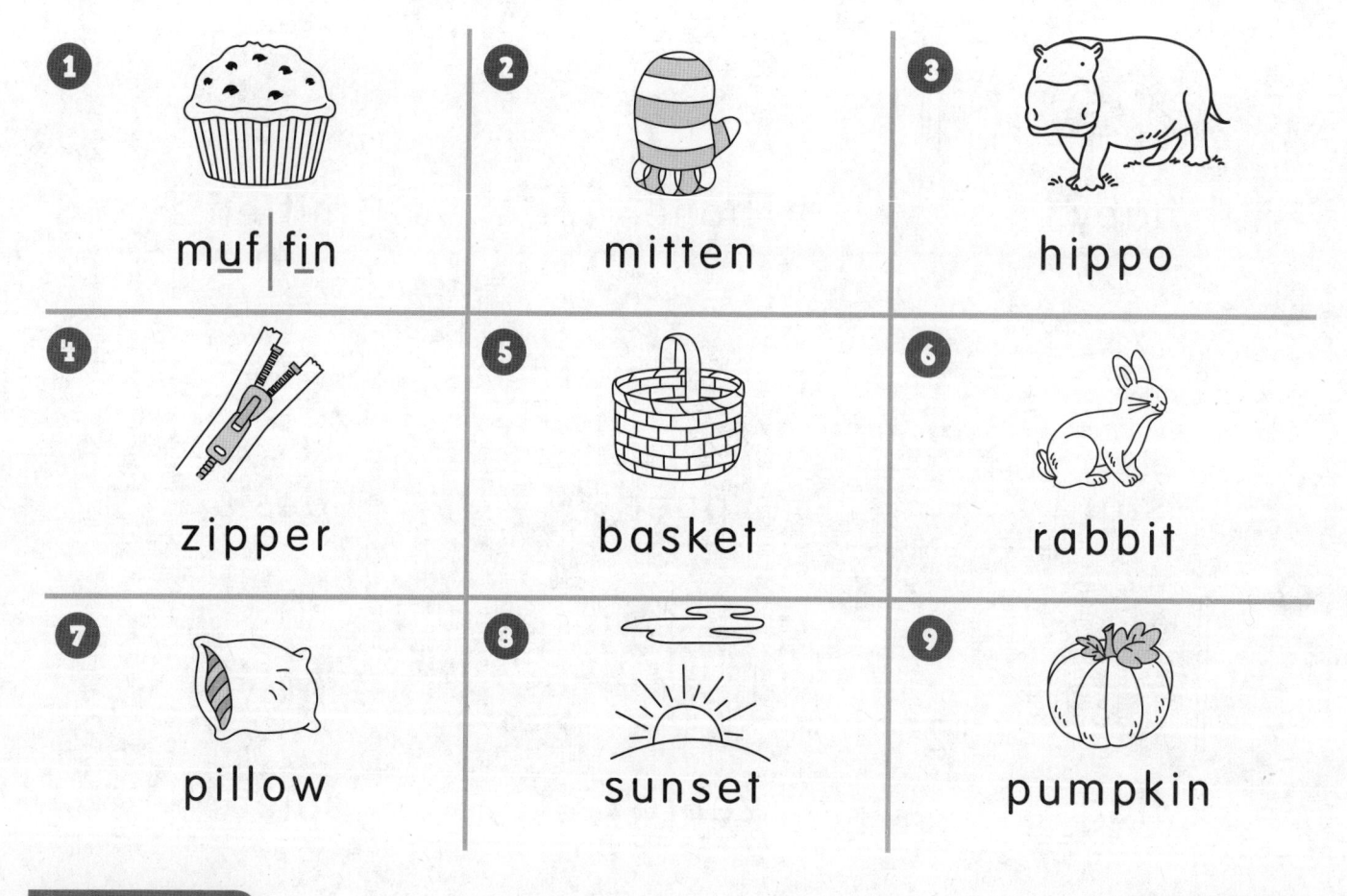

1. muf | fin
2. mitten
3. hippo
4. zipper
5. basket
6. rabbit
7. pillow
8. sunset
9. pumpkin

Dictation

Read It

Day 3 | Week 9

Focus: Many words are divided between a vowel and a consonant. When the first vowel sound is **long**, divide the word after the vowel.

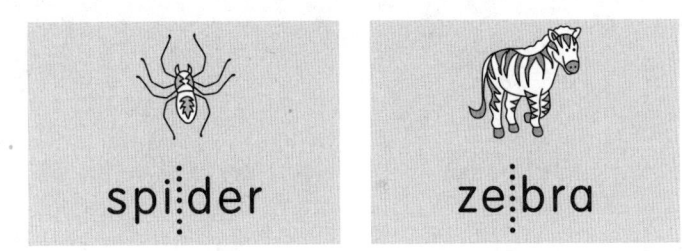

spi|der   ze|bra

Divide the word into syllables. Circle the vowel that has the **long** sound.

1 tulip

2 pony

3 robot

4 paper

5 music

6 baby

Dictation

___ ___ ___ ___ ___ ___ ___ ___ ___ □

© Evan-Moor Corp. • EMC 6772 • Daily Phonics

43

Read It

Day 4 | Week 9

Focus — Many words are divided between a consonant and a vowel. When the first vowel sound is **short**, divide the word after the consonant.

cab|in   med|al

Divide the word into syllables. Underline the **first** vowel.

1. lemon
2. camel
3. seven
4. wizard
5. robin
6. shovel

Dictation ....

_____ _____ _____ _____ _____ _____ ☐

Write It

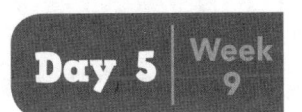

Day 5 | Week 9

Word Box

lemon	pony	mitten	robot
muffin	music	basket	robin
pillow	seven	baby	shovel

Write each word under the rule it follows.

ten:nis
Divide between two consonants.

_____
_____
_____
_____

ze:bra
When the first vowel sound is **long**, divide after the vowel.

_____
_____
_____
_____

cab:in
When the first vowel is **short**, divide after the consonant.

_____
_____
_____
_____

Dictation

___ ___ ___ ___ ___ ___ ___ ___

Listen for It

Day 1 | Week 10

Focus The letter **y** can have the **long i** or the **long e** sound.

y = long i
cry

y = long e
puppy

Say the picture name. Read the word.
What sound does the **y** have? Fill in the circle next to **long i** or **long e**.

1. pony — ○ long i ○ long e

2. sky — ○ long i ○ long e

3. bunny — ○ long i ○ long e

4. forty — ○ long i ○ long e

5. spy — ○ long i ○ long e

6. lady — ○ long i ○ long e

7. baby — ○ long i ○ long e

8. fry — ○ long i ○ long e

9. fly — ○ long i ○ long e

Dictation

1. ____ ____ ____   2. ____ ____ ____   3. ____ ____ ____

46 Daily Phonics • EMC 6772 • © Evan-Moor Corp.

Listen for It

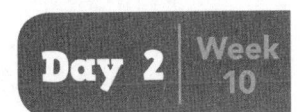

Day 2 | Week 10

Focus: Y has the **long i** sound in words with 1 syllable.
Y has the **long e** sound in words with 2 syllables.

cry	**1** syllable

puppy	**2** syllables

Say the picture name. Listen to the syllables.
Fill in the circle next to the number that shows how many syllables you hear.
Then fill in the circle next to **i** or **e** to show what sound the **y** has.

1. sunny — syllable: ○ 1 ○ 2 — y: ○ i ○ e

2. fly — syllable: ○ 1 ○ 2 — y: ○ i ○ e

3. baby — syllable: ○ 1 ○ 2 — y: ○ i ○ e

4. pony — syllable: ○ 1 ○ 2 — y: ○ i ○ e

5. spy — syllable: ○ 1 ○ 2 — y: ○ i ○ e

6. sky — syllable: ○ 1 ○ 2 — y: ○ i ○ e

Dictation

1. ____ ____ ____ ____

2. ____ ____ ____ ____

Write It

Day 3 | Week 10

Word Box

shy	forty	lady
fry	dry	hungry
happy	my	try

Read each word. Does the **y** have the **long i** or **long e** sound? Write the word in the correct box.

y = long i	**y = long e**
_____	_____
_____	_____
_____	_____
_____	_____
_____	_____

Dictation

1. ____ ____   2. ____ ____ ____   3. ____ ____ ____ ____ ____

Read It

Day 4 | Week 10

Read the sentence. Draw a line to the correct picture.

1 My cat is **hungry**.

2 What is up in the **sky**?

3 May I pet the **pony**?

4 Do not make the girl **cry**.

5 The **puppy** is **happy**.

6 The bird can **fly**.

Dictation

Read It

Day 5 | Week 10

Write the missing words. Then read the sentence.

1

hungry   pony

She fed the _____ _____.

2

puppy   lady

The _____ has a pet _____.

3

sunny   bunny

The _____ likes a _____ day.

4

pony   fly

The _____ sat on the _____.

Dictation ··

_____

Listen for It

Day 1 | Week 11

| Focus | Two consonant sounds said together are called a **consonant blend**. |

| st | sk | sw | sp |
| **st**ir | **sk**y | **sw**am | **sp**ill |

Say the sound of the blend. Then say the picture name.
Fill in the circle if the picture name begins with that blend.

1. st-
2. sk-
3. sw-
4. sp-

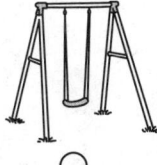

Dictation

1. _____ ay   2. _____ ip   3. _____ amp

© Evan-Moor Corp. • EMC 6772 • Daily Phonics

51

Listen for It

Day 2 | Week 11

Focus — Two consonant sounds said together are called a **consonant blend**.

st	sk	sw	sp
stir	**sk**y	**sw**am	**sp**ill

Say the picture name.
Fill in the circle next to the blend you hear.

1. ○ sp ○ sk ○ st

2. ○ sp ○ sk ○ st

3. ○ sp ○ sk ○ st

4. ○ sw ○ sp ○ sk

5. ○ sw ○ sp ○ sk

6. ○ sw ○ sp ○ sk

7. ○ sp ○ sk ○ st

8. ○ sp ○ sk ○ st

9. ○ sp ○ sk ○ st

Dictation

1. ___ ___ ill   2. ___ ___ an   3. ___ ___ ipe

Write It

Day 3 — Week 11

Blend Box

st   sk   sw   sp

Say the picture name. Listen to the letter-sounds.
Write the blend to spell the word.

1 ___ ___ate

2 ___ ___ing

3 ___ ___y

4 ___ ___ar

5 ___ ___oon

6 ___ ___im

7 ___ ___unk

8 ___ ___eep

9 ___ ___amp

Dictation

1. ___ ___ep   2. ___ ___ill   3. ___ ___ell

© Evan-Moor Corp. • EMC 6772 • Daily Phonics   53

Write It

Day 4 | Week 11

Word Box

skip	stamp	swan	skin
step	skate	spit	spell
swim	spot	swipe	star

Read each word in the word box. Write the word under the correct letters.

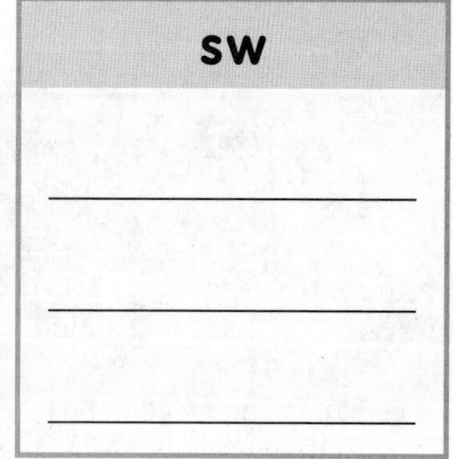

st

sk

sw

sp

Dictation

1. ___ ___ar   2. ___ ___ine   3. ___ ___em

Read It

Day 5 | Week 11

Write the missing words. Then read the sentence.

1. stars   space

I look up into _____ and see the _____.

2. swing   skunk

The _____ likes to _____.

3. spoon   sponge

I use a _____ to wash the _____.

4. skirt   sweater

I have a _____ and a _____.

Dictation

Listen for It

Day 1 | Week 12

Focus: Two consonant sounds said together are called a **consonant blend**.

fl	gl	sl	pl
flag	**gl**obe	**sl**ed	**pl**ate

Say the sound of the blend. Then say the picture name.
Fill in the circle if the picture name begins with that blend.

1. fl-
2. gl-
3. sl-
4. pl-

Dictation

1. _____ ip   2. _____ ad   3. _____ am

Write It

Day 2 | Week 12

Blend Box

fl   gl   sl   pl

Say the picture name. Listen to the letter-sounds.
Write the blend to spell the word.

1. ___ ___ass
2. ___ ___ide
3. ___ ___ane
4. ___ ___ower
5. ___ ___ate
6. ___ ___obe
7. ___ ___ag
8. ___ ___ant
9. ___ ___ed

Dictation

1. ___ ___ap   2. ___ ___ow   3. ___ ___ap

Listen for It

Day 3 | Week 12

Focus: Two consonant sounds said together are called a **consonant blend**.

cr	fr	tr	gr
crib	**fr**ame	**tr**ee	**gr**ill

Say the sound of the blend. Then say each picture name.
Fill in the circle if the picture name begins with that blend.

1 cr-

2 fr-

3 tr-

4 gr-

Dictation

1. _____ _____ ab
2. _____ _____ og
3. _____ _____ ap

Write It

Day 4 | Week 12

Blend Box
cr fr tr gr

Say the picture name. Listen to the letter-sounds.
Write the blend to spell the word.

1.  ___ ___ee
2.  ___ ___ass
3.  ___ ___og
4.  ___ ___ab
5.  ___ ___apes
6.  ___ ___uck
7.  ___ ___ain
8.  ___ ___ame
9.  ___ ___own

Dictation

1. ___ ___ay
2. ___ ___ow
3. ___ ___ip

Read It

Day 5 | Week 12

Write the missing words. Then read the sentence.

1

plate   crab

The _____ is on the _____.

2

grows   tree   flower

The _____ _____ under the _____.

3

frog   slide   green

The _____ _____ slid down the _____.

Dictation ....

Listen for It

Day 1 | Week 13

Focus: Two consonant sounds said together are called a **consonant blend**. Many words end with a consonant blend.

lt	st	nt	mp
me**lt**	li**st**	de**nt**	ra**mp**

Say the sound of the blend. Then say the picture name.
Fill in the circle if the picture name **ends** with that sound.

1 -lt

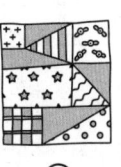

2 -st

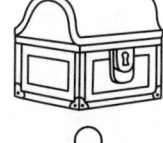

3 -nt

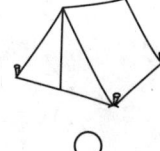

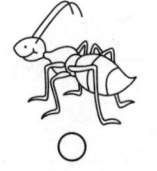

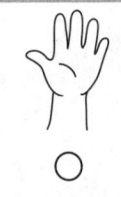

4 -mp

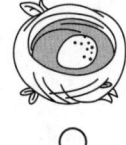

Dictation

1. re____   2. li____   3. pu____

Write It

Day 2 | Week 13

Blend Box

lt　　st　　nt　　mp

Say the picture name. Write the blend to spell the word. Then read the word.

1.  qui___ ___

2. 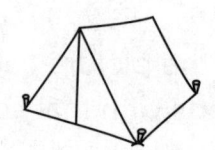 te___ ___

3. 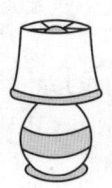 la___ ___

4.  gho___ ___

5.  sta___ ___

6.  pla___ ___

7.  be___ ___

8.  che___ ___

9.  ne___ ___

Dictation ....

1. me___ ___　　2. ca___ ___　　3. mi___ ___

Listen for It

Day 3 | Week 13

Focus: Two consonant sounds said together are called a **consonant blend**. Many words end with a consonant blend.

nd	ft	ld	nk
me**nd**	lo**ft**	ba**ld**	ta**nk**

Say the sound of the blend. Then say the picture name.
Fill in the circle if the picture name **ends** with that sound.

1. -nd

2. -ft

3. -ld

4. -nk

Dictation

1. co___ ___   2. le___ ___   3. la___ ___

Write It

Day 4 | Week 13

Blend Box

nd ft ld nk

Say the picture name. Write the blend to spell the word.
Then read the word.

1. ra___ ___
2. wi___ ___
3. go___ ___
4. ha___ ___
5. sku___ ___
6. co___ ___
7. gi___ ___
8. ba___ ___
9. ta___ ___

Dictation

1. bu___ ___
2. wa___ ___
3. li___ ___

Read It

Day 5 | Week 13

Write the missing words. Then read the sentence.

1. raft   ant   nest

The _____ is on the _____.

2.  lamp   nest   skunk

The _____ is in the _____.

3.  tent   plant   band

The _____ plays in a _____.

4.  quilt   chest   gold

The _____ is in the _____.

Dictation ··

_____

© Evan-Moor Corp. • EMC 6772 • Daily Phonics

Listen for It

Day 1 | Week 14

Focus: A **digraph** is two letters together that have one sound. Many words begin with a digraph.

sh	ch	wh	th
shed	**ch**est	**wh**ip	**th**orn

Say the sound of the two letters. Then say each picture name.
Fill in the circle if the picture name begins with that sound.

1. sh-
2. ch-
3. wh-
4. th-

Dictation

1. ___ ___ in   2. ___ ___ ink   3. ___ ___ ovel

Write It

Day 2 | Week 14

Letter Box

sh   ch   wh   th

Say the picture name. Listen to the first sound.
Write the missing letters to spell the word.

1. ___ ___ell

2. ___ ___ick

3. ___ ___read

4. ___ ___erry

5. ___ ___irt

6. ___ ___ale

7. ___ ___ree

8. ___ ___eel

9. ___ ___ain

Dictation

1. ___ ___art   2. ___ ___elf   3. ___ ___ank

Listen for It

Day 3 | Week 14

Focus: A **digraph** is two letters together that have one sound. Many words end with a digraph.

sh	ch	th
pu**sh**	in**ch**	pa**th**

Say the sound of the two letters. Then say each picture name.
Fill in the circle if the picture name **ends** with that sound.

1 -sh

2 -ch

3 -th

Dictation

1. ma____ ____   2. mu____ ____   3. fre____ ____

Write It

Day 4 | Week 14

Letter Box

sh   ch   th

Say the picture name. Listen to the **last** sound.
Write the missing letters to spell the word.

1. 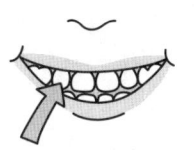 tee___ ___
2.  fi___ ___
3.  wat___ ___
4.  lea___ ___
5.  pea___ ___
6. ma___ ___
7.  ben___ ___
8.  ba___ ___
9.  wa___ ___

Dictation

1. lun___ ___   2. ma___ ___   3. bo___ ___

Read It

Day 5 | Week 14

Read the sentence. Underline the consonant digraph. Then draw a line to the correct picture.

1. Put food into the cat's **dish**.

2. **Whales** are big animals.

3. Give the dog a **bath**.

4. A **sheep** is in the pen.

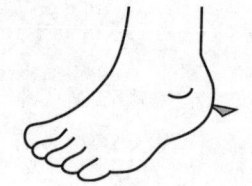

5. He had a **thorn** in his foot.

6. There is a **bench** in the park.

Dictation ....

Listen for It

Day 1 | Week 15

Focus: A **digraph** is two letters together that have one sound. The digraphs **ph** and **gh** have the /f/ sound.

| ph |  📱 | **ph**one | gh |  👧 | lau**gh** |

Say the picture name. Listen to the letter-sounds. Underline the letters that stand for the /f/ sound.

1.  gopher
2.  cough
3.  trophy
4. 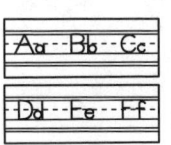 alphabet
5.  elephant
6. 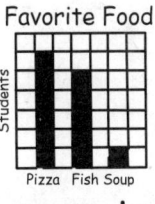 graph
7.  rough
8.  dolphin
9.  photo

Dictation

1. go____ ____er   2. cou____ ____

Write It

Day 2 | Week 15

Word Box

alphabet	cough	trophy
phone	rough	laugh
gopher	elephant	enough

Read each word in the word box. Does it have **ph** or **gh**?
Write the word under the correct letters.

/f/ = ph	/f/ = gh
_____	_____
_____	_____
_____	_____
_____	_____
_____	_____

Dictation ....

1. tou____ 2. gra____ 3. enou____

Listen for It

Day 3 | Week 15

Focus: A **digraph** is two letters together that have one sound. Many words end with a digraph.

| ck |  👦 | ba**ck** | ng | 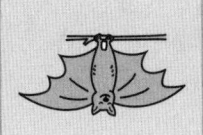 🦇 | ha**ng** |

Say the picture name. Listen to the **last** letter-sound.
Fill in the circle next to the letters that stand for that sound.

1. 
○ ck
○ ng

2. 
○ ck
○ ng

3. 
○ ck
○ ng

4. 
○ ck
○ ng

5. 
○ ck
○ ng

6. 
○ ck
○ ng

7. 
○ ck
○ ng

8. 
○ ck
○ ng

9. 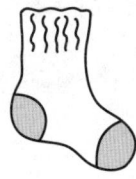
○ ck
○ ng

Dictation

1. blo___ ___   2. bri___ ___   3. ki___ ___

Write It

Day 4 | Week 15

Letter Box

ck   ng

Say the picture name. Listen to the **last** sound.
Write the missing letters to spell the word.

1. ki____ ____

2. clo____ ____

3. du____ ____

4. swi____ ____

5. tru____ ____

6. si____ ____

7. bri____ ____

8. so____ ____

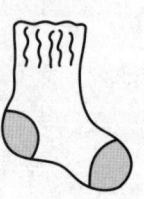

9. ri____ ____

Dictation

1. spri____ ____

2. pa____ ____

3. lo____ ____

Read It

Day 5 | Week 15

Write the missing words. Then read the sentence.

1. wing   duck

The _____ hurt its _____.

2. trophy   king

The _____ won a _____.

3. sang   alphabet

The boy _____ the _____.

4. chick   laugh

Did she _____ at the _____?

Dictation

1. ne____ ____   2. sti____ ____   3. ____ ____one

Listen for It

Day 1 | Week 16

Focus: When a vowel is followed by the letter r, it changes the sound of the vowel.

st**ar**    f**or**k

Say the picture name.
Fill in the circle next to the letters that stand for the vowel +r sound you hear.

1. ○ or ○ ar
2. ○ or ○ ar
3. ○ or ○ ar
4. ○ or ○ ar
5. ○ or ○ ar
6. ○ or ○ ar
7. ○ or ○ ar
8. ○ or ○ ar
9. ○ or ○ ar

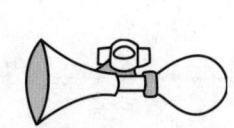

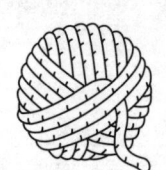

Dictation

1. h___ ___d   2. f___ ___t   3. t___ ___t

Write It

Day 2 | **Week 16**

Letter Box

ar   or

Say the picture name. Listen to the letter-sounds.
Write the letters to spell the word.

1. b __ __ n

2. c __ __ n

3. f __ __ k

4. g __ __ den

5. sh __ __ k

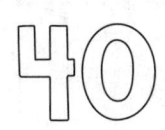

6. h __ __ n

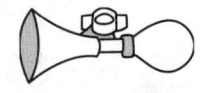

7. f __ __ ty

8. sc __ __ f

9. y __ __ n

Dictation

1. __ __ m   2. th __ __ n   3. d __ __ t

Listen for It

Day 3 | Week 16

Focus: The letters **ur**, **er**, and **ir** have the same sound: /ur/.

ur	er	ir
s**ur**f	cl**er**k	st**ir**

Say the picture name. Read the word.
Underline the letters that have the /ur/ sound.

1. turtle
2. shirt
3. purse
4. letter
5. nurse
6. bird
7. water
8. skirt
9. turkey

Dictation

1. ___ir___   2. ___ur___   3. lett_____

Write It

Day 4 | Week 16

Word Box

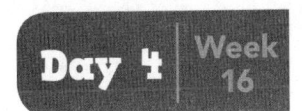

turkey	clerk	nurse	herd
bird	curb	water	birth
fern	shirt	stir	purse

Read each word in the Word Box. Does it have **ur**, **er**, or **ir**?
Write the word under the correct letters.

ur	er	ir

Dictation ....

Read It

Day 5 | Week 16

Read the sentence. Then draw a line to the matching picture.

1 My dad honked the car horn.

2 I plant corn in the garden.

3 The shark swims in water.

4 A turkey is a bird.

5 My shirt is torn.

6 I put on a scarf at the store.

Dictation ··

1. ____ ____ ____   2. ____ ____ ____ ____

Listen for It

Day 1 | Week 17

Focus: The letter **c** has two sounds. It can have the **/k/** sound you hear in **cup**. This is called the **hard c** sound. It can have the **/s/** sound you hear in **city**. This is called the **soft c** sound.

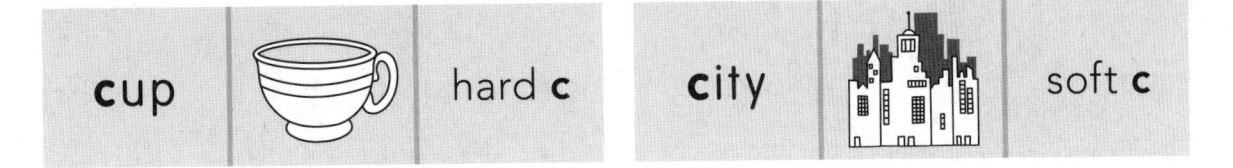

| cup | hard c | city | soft c |

Say the picture name. Listen to the sound of **c**.
Fill in the circle below **hard c** or **soft c**.

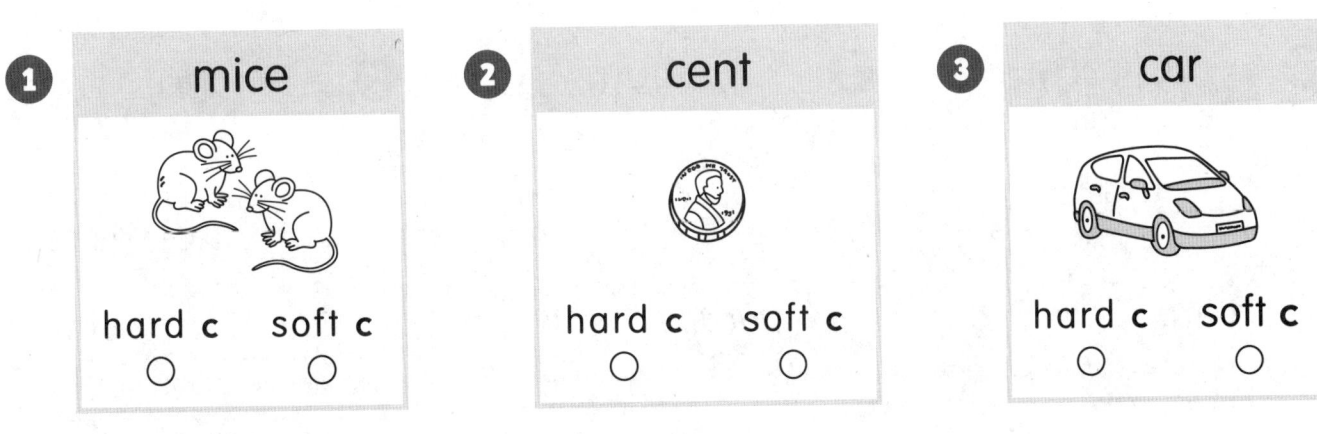

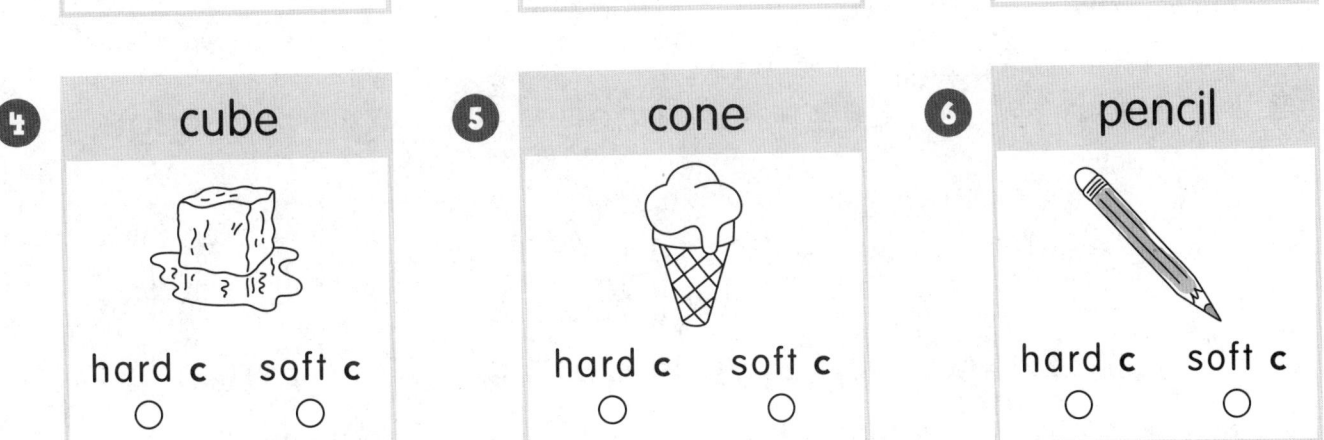

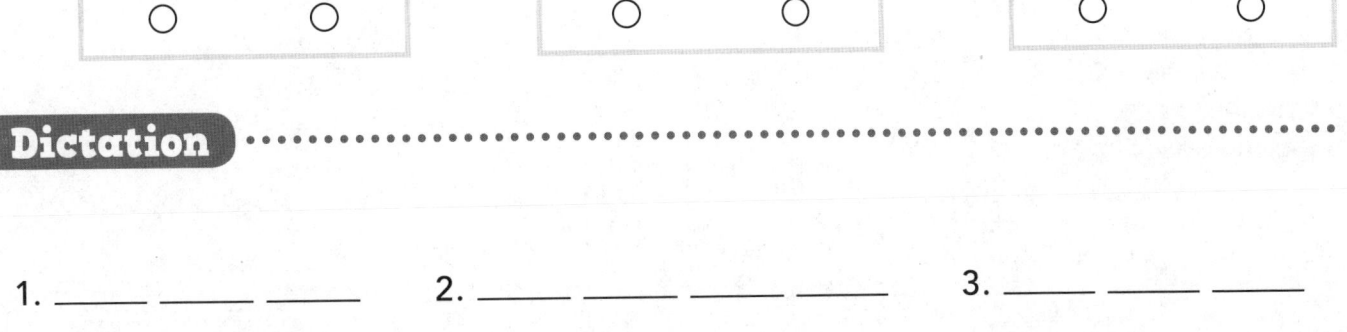

1. mice — hard c soft c

2. cent — hard c soft c

3. car — hard c soft c

4. cube — hard c soft c

5. cone — hard c soft c

6. pencil — hard c soft c

Dictation

1. ___ ___ ___   2. ___ ___ ___   3. ___ ___ ___

Listen for It

Day 2 | Week 17

Focus: The letter **g** has two sounds. It can have the /g/ sound you hear in **gas**. This is called the **hard g** sound. It can have the /j/ sound you hear in **general**. This is called the **soft g** sound.

| **g**as |  hard **g** | **g**eneral |  soft **g** |

Say the picture name. Listen to the sound of **g**.
Fill in the circle below **hard g** or **soft g**.

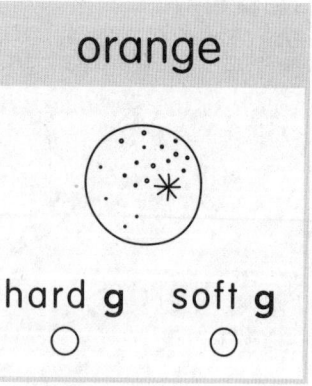

1. giraffe — hard g ○ soft g ○

2. gum — hard g ○ soft g ○

3. gate — hard g ○ soft g ○

4. orange — hard g ○ soft g ○

5. goat — hard g ○ soft g ○

6. cage — hard g ○ soft g ○

Dictation

1. ____ ____ ____ ____   2. ____ ____ ____

Write It

Day 3 | Week 17

Word Box

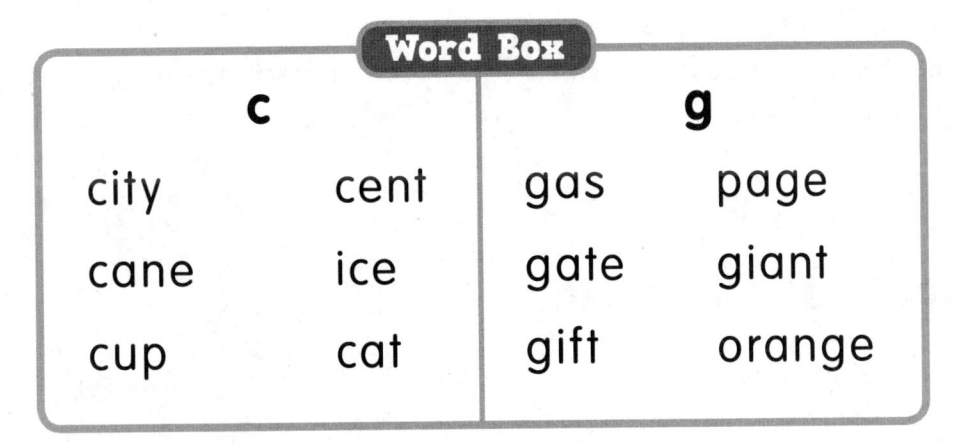

c		g	
city	cent	gas	page
cane	ice	gate	giant
cup	cat	gift	orange

Read each word in the Word Box. Listen to the sound of **c** or **g**. Write the word under the correct sound.

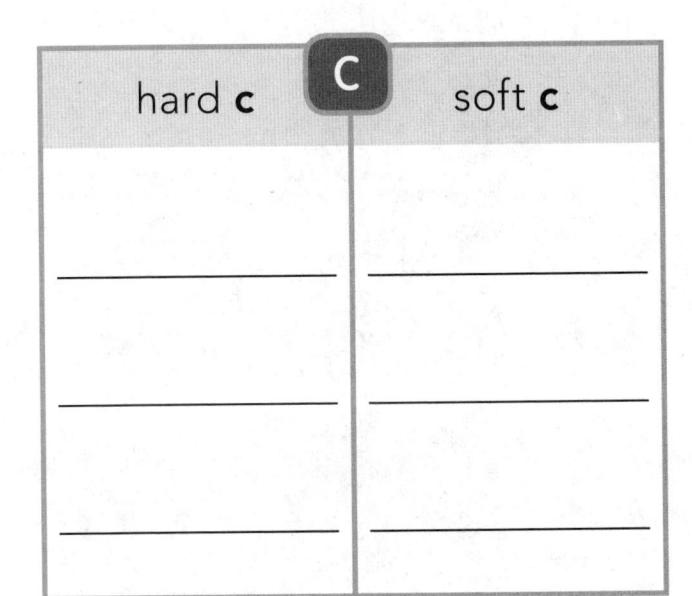

hard **c**	soft **c**

hard **g**	soft **g**

Dictation

1. _____ _____ _____ _____

2. _____ _____ _____ _____ _____

Read It

Day 4 | Week 17

Read the sentence. Then read the underlined word.
Fill in the circle to show if you hear a **hard** or a **soft** letter-sound.

	hard	soft
1. The goat sat on my car.	○	○
2. The mice ate the rice.	○	○
3. The gum is white.	○	○
4. Put the ice in the cup.	○	○
5. The car has gas in it.	○	○
6. The giraffe is orange.	○	○

Dictation ....

1. _____ _____   2. _____ _____ _____   3. _____ _____ _____

Read It

Day 5 | Week 17

Write the missing words. Then read the sentence.

1   cave   cub

The _____ hid in the _____.

2   cage   mice

I see _____ in a _____.

3   gate   garden

Open the _____ _____.

4   rice   corn

I like _____ and _____.

Dictation ....

Listen for It

Day 1 | Week 18

Focus: The **long a** sound can be spelled **ai** or **ay**.
The letters **ai** usually appear in the middle of a word.
The letters **ay** usually appear at the end of a word.

ch**ai**n

tr**ay**

Say the picture name.
Underline the letters that stand for the **long a** sound.

1. rain
2. hay
3. snail
4. nail
5. pay
6. train
7. spray
8. mail
9. pail

Dictation

1. _____ _____

2. _____ _____ _____ _____

86   Daily Phonics • EMC 6772 • © Evan-Moor Corp.

Write It

Day 2 | Week 18

Word Box

snail	tray	chain
spray	rain	hay
train	nail	pail

Say the picture name. Write the word on the line.
Circle the letters that have the **long a** sound.

1. _____
2. _____
3. _____
4. _____
5. _____
6. _____
7. _____
8. _____
9. _____

Dictation

1. ___ ai ___   2. ___ ai ___   3. ___ ___ ay

Write It

Day 3 | Week 18

Word Box

stay	rail	play	nail
paint	grain	maid	jay
clay	spray	mail	hay

Read each word in the Word Box. Write the word under the correct letters.

ay at the end	**ai** in the middle
_____	_____
_____	_____
_____	_____
_____	_____
_____	_____
_____	_____

Dictation

1. ____ ____ ____ ____ ____

2. ____ ____ ____ ____ ____

Read It

Day 4 | Week 18

Read the words. Underline the letters that have the **long a** sound. Then draw a line to the correct picture.

1. little **snail**

2. wet **rain**

3. soft **clay**

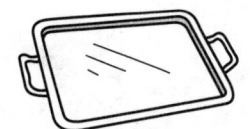

4. red **paint**

5. **spray** can

6. lunch **tray**

Dictation

1. _____ _____ _____ _____ _____   2. _____ _____ _____

Read It

Day 5 | Week 18

Write the missing words. Then read the sentence.

1   hay   nail

There is a _____ in the _____.

2   rain   train

The _____ fell on the _____.

3   pail   play

Ray likes to _____ with his _____.

4   snail   jay   tray

A _____ and a _____ sat on a _____.

Dictation ···

90   Daily Phonics • EMC 6772 • © Evan-Moor Corp.

Listen for It

Day 1 | Week 19

Focus: A **vowel digraph** is two vowels together that have one sound. The digraphs spelled **ee** and **ea** can have the **long e** sound.

j**ee**p

wh**ea**t

Say the picture name. Then read the word.
Underline the letters that stand for the **long e** sound.

1. tree
2. bean
3. peach
4. wheel
5. queen
6. bee
7. beak
8. pea
9. sheep

Dictation

1. ____ ____ ____ ____   2. ____ ____ ____

Write It

Day 2 | Week 19

Word Box

sheep	bee	pea
feet	beak	jeep
wheel	seal	sleep

Say the picture name. Write the word on the line.
Then circle the letters that have the **long e** sound.

1. _____

2. _____

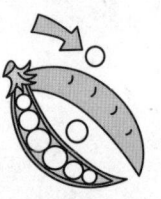

3. _____

4. _____

5. _____

6. _____

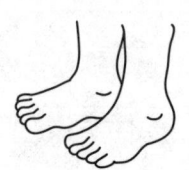

7. _____

8. _____

9. _____

Dictation ....

1. ___ ee ___   2. ___ ea ___   3. ___ ee ___

Write It

Day 3 | Week 19

Word Box

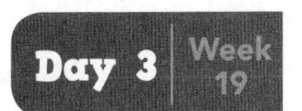

cheek	wheat	tree	sweet
meat	seal	feet	teach
sleep	keep	read	peach

Read each word in the Word Box. Write the word under the correct letters.

ee	ea
_____	_____
_____	_____
_____	_____
_____	_____
_____	_____
_____	_____

Dictation

_____

Read It

Day 4 | **Week 19**

Read the words. Underline the letters that have the **long e** sound.
Then draw a line to the correct picture.

1. two **feet**

2. big **bee**

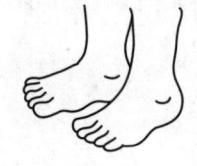

3. little **bean**

4. black **wheel**

5. soft **peach**

6. tall **tree**

Dictation

1. ___ ___ ___ ___   2. ___ ___ ___ ___

Read It

Day 5 | Week 19

Write the missing words. Then read the sentence.

1   tree   bee

There is a _____ in the _____.

2   beak   sheep

A _____ does not have a _____!

3   sweet   peach

The _____ is soft and _____.

4   jeep   seat

I will sit in the front _____ of the _____.

Dictation ··

Listen for It

Day 1 | Week 20

Focus: The **long i** sound can be spelled **ie** or **igh**.
The letters **ie** can have the /ī/ sound you hear in **lie**.
The letters **igh** have the /ī/ sound you hear in **right**.

lie

right

Say the picture name. Then read the word.
Underline the letters that stand for the **long i** sound.

1. light
2. pie
3. night
4. high
5. fight
6. fried
7. tie
8. cries
9. thigh

Dictation

1. ____ ____ ____   2. ____ ____ ____   3. ____ ____ ____ ____

Write It

Day 2 | Week 20

Word Box

cries	pie	thigh
light	fight	night
tie	fried	high

Say the picture name. Write the word on the line.
Then circle the letters that have the **long i** sound.

1.
2.
3.

4.
5.
6.

7.
8.
9.

Dictation

1. ___ igh   2. ___ ___ ied   3. ___ ___ ies

Write It

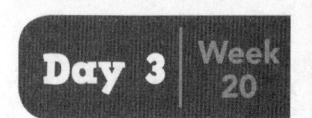

Day 3 | Week 20

Word Box

tried	cries	pie	night
high	right	light	fried
lie	bright	tie	thigh

Read each word in the Word Box. Write the word under the correct letters.

ie	igh
_____	_____
_____	_____
_____	_____
_____	_____
_____	_____
_____	_____

Dictation ••

Read It

Day 4 | Week 20

Read the words. Underline the letters that stand for the **long i** sound. Then draw a line to the correct picture.

1. peach **pie**

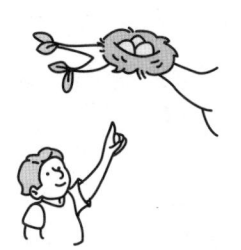

2. dark **night**

3. red **tie**

4. up **high**

5. **fried** egg

6. baby **cries**

Dictation

1. ____ ____ ____ ____

2. ____ ____ ____ ____

Read It

Day 5 | Week 20

Write the missing words. Then read the sentence.

1. thigh   fried

Mom _____ the chicken _____.

2. night   cries

The baby _____ at _____.

3. high   tie

I can _____ the rope up _____.

4. light   night   bright

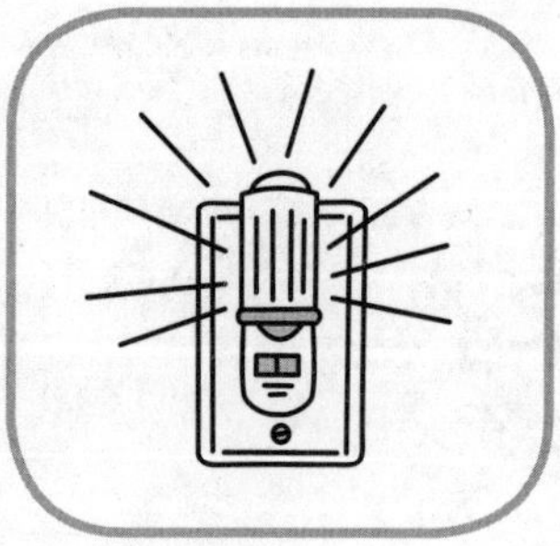

My _____ _____ is so _____.

Dictation ....

Listen for It

Day 1 | Week 21

Focus: A vowel digraph is two vowels together that have one sound. The digraphs **oa**, **oe**, and **ow** can have the **long o** sound.

c**oa**t   J**oe**   r**ow**

Say the picture name. Then read the word.
Underline the letters that stand for the **long o** sound.

1. 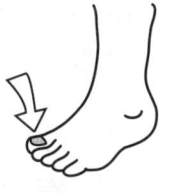 toe
2.  snow
3.  boat
4.  bow
5.  goat
6.  hoe
7.  toad
8.  mow
9.  tow

Dictation

1. _____ _____ _____ _____   2. _____ _____ _____ _____   3. _____ _____ _____ _____

© Evan-Moor Corp. • EMC 6772 • Daily Phonics

101

Write It

Day 2 | Week 21

Word Box

blow	Joe	toe
boat	crow	mow
hoe	goat	coat

Say the picture name. Write the word on the line.
Then circle the letters that have the **long o** sound.

1. _____

2. _____

3. _____

4. _____

5. _____

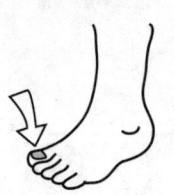

6. _____

7. _____

8. _____

9. _____

Dictation ••

1. ____ oa ____   2. ____ ow   3. ____ oa ____

102   Daily Phonics • EMC 6772 • © Evan-Moor Corp.

Write It

Day 3 | Week 21

Word Box

row	road	mow	toe
toad	doe	glow	coach
Joe	crow	goat	hoe

Read each word in the Word Box. Write the word under the correct letters.

oa	oe	ow
_____	_____	_____
_____	_____	_____
_____	_____	_____
_____	_____	_____

Dictation ....

1. ____ ____ ____   2. ____ ____ ____   3. ____ ____ ____ ____

Read It

Day 4 | Week 21

Read the words. Underline the letters that stand for the **long o** sound. Then draw a line to the correct picture.

1. **tow** a car

2. cold **snow**

3. big **toe**

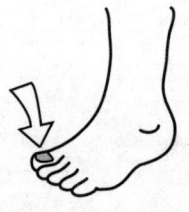

4. pretty **bow**

5. little **boat**

6. warm **coat**

Dictation ....

1. _____   2. _____   3. _____

Read It

Day 5 | Week 21

Write the missing words. Then read the sentence.

1.  toe   bow

I put a _____ on my big _____.

2.  Joe   coat

I see _____ in his warm _____.

3.  road   goat

The _____ is in the _____.

4.  boat   row

_____ the _____ on the lake.

Dictation ··

Listen for It

Day 1 | Week 22

Focus: A vowel digraph is two vowels together that have one sound. The digraphs **ue** and **ew** can have the **long u** sound.

gl**ue**

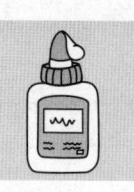

fl**ew**

Say the picture name. Then read the word.
Underline the letters that stand for the **long u** sound.

1.  blew
2.  Sue
3.  new
4.  jewel
5.  stew
6.  clue
7.  screw
8.  blue
9.  grew

Dictation

1. _____ 2. _____ 3. _____

Write It

Day 2 — Week 22

Word Box

clue	stew	grew
flew	blue	jewel
Sue	glue	screw

Say the picture name. Write the word on the line.
Then circle the letters that have the **long u** sound.

1. _____ 
2. _____ 
3. _____ 
4. _____ 
5. _____ 
6. _____ 
7. _____ 
8. _____ 
9. _____

Dictation

1. _____   2. _____   3. _____

Write It

Day 3 | Week 22

Word Box

clue	blue	glue
stew	flew	screw
new	true	chew

Read each word in the Word Box. Write the word under the correct letters.

ue	ew
_____	_____
_____	_____
_____	_____
_____	_____

Dictation

1. _____   2. _____   3. _____

Read It

Day 4 | Week 22

Read the words. Underline the letters that stand for the **long u** sound. Then draw a line to the correct picture.

1. **new** pants

2. birds **flew**

3. **true** story

4. **blue** dress

5. big **jewel**

6. white **glue**

Dictation

1. _____   2. _____   3. _____

Read It

Day 5 | Week 22

Write the missing words. Then read the sentence.

1. new   chew

The dog likes to _____ on my _____ sock.

2. clue   Sue

_____ found a _____.

3. grew   blew

The plant _____ and the wind _____.

4. jewel   blue

I have a _____ _____.

Dictation ....

_____

Listen for It

Day 1 | Week 23

Focus: Many letter pairs stand for **long** vowel sounds.

long **a**	long **e**	long **i**	long **o**	long **u**
ai ay	ee ea	ie igh	oa ow	ew ue

Say the picture name. Then read the word.
Underline the letters that stand for the **long** vowel sound.

1. tree
2. hay
3. tie
4. mow
5. train
6. pea
7. light
8. boat
9. glue

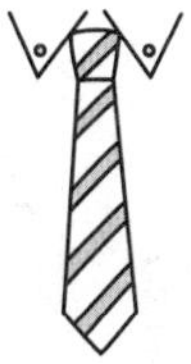

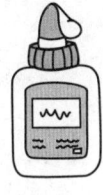

Dictation

1. _____ 2. _____ 3. _____

Write It

Day 2 | Week 23

Word Box

snail	night	sheep
beak	screw	clue
toad	tray	pie

Say the picture name. Write the word on the line.
Then circle the letters that have the **long** vowel sound.

1. _____
2. _____
3. _____
4. _____
5. _____
6. _____
7. _____
8. _____
9. _____

Dictation

1. _____ 2. _____ 3. _____

Write It

Day 3 | Week 23

Word Box

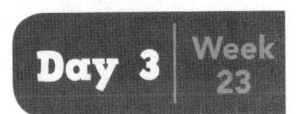

paint	chew	snow	true
slow	bean	high	pie
spray	nail	feet	toad

Read each word in the Word Box. Write the word under the correct **long** vowel.

long a
ai   ay

long e
ee   ea

long i
ie   igh

long o
oa   ow

long u
ew   ue

Dictation

Write It

Day 4 | Week 23

Letter Box

ai   ee   oa   ie   ue   ow

Say the picture name. Listen to the vowel sound.
Write the letters that stand for that sound.

1. qu____ ____n

2. gl____ ____

3. ch____ ____n

4. t____ ____

5. r____ ____n

6. c____ ____t

7. p____ ____

8. cl____ ____

9. sn____ ____

Dictation ....

Read It

Day 5 | Week 23

Read the incomplete sentence. Write the correct word on the line. Then read the sentence again.

1. The _____ moved slowly on the trail.
   snail   snow

2. The _____ is tall and green.
   tree   tray

3. Turn the _____ off when you go.
   lie   light

4. Look at that big _____!
   new   jewel

5. Take your _____ to the beach.
   pail   rain

6. Joe has a pet _____.
   goat   tow

Dictation

Listen for It

Day 1 | Week 24

Focus: The letter pairs **ou** and **ow** both can have the vowel sound you hear in **cow**.

| r**ou**nd | ◯ | d**ow**n | ⬇ |

Say the picture name. Then read the word.
Underline the letters that stand for the vowel sound in **cow**.

1. mouth	2. clown	3. towel
4. house	5. mouse	6. crown
7. scout	8. cloud	9. owl

Dictation

1. _____   2. _____   3. _____

Write It

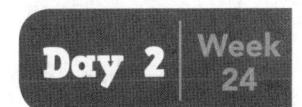

Day 2 | Week 24

Word Box

owl	mouse	house
cloud	towel	clown
mouth	scout	crown

Say the picture name. Write the word on the line.
Then circle the letters that stand for the vowel sound in **cow**.

1.
2.
3.
4.
5.
6.
7.
8.
9.

Dictation ....

Write It

Day 3 | **Week 24**

Word Box

shout	house	cow
crowd	gown	brown
sound	couch	count

Read each word in the Word Box. Write the word under the correct letters.

ou	ow

Dictation ....

Read It

Day 4 | Week 24

Read the words. Underline the letters that stand for the vowel sound in **cow**. Then draw a line to the correct picture.

1. cute **mouse**

2. night **owl**

3. funny **clown**

4. fluffy **cloud**

5. black and white **cow**

6. boy **scout**

Dictation

Read It

Day 5 | Week 24

Write the missing words. Then read the sentence.

1   sound   scout

The _____ did not make a _____.

2   house   owl

The _____ sat on the _____.

3   towel   mouse

A _____ is on the _____.

4   brown   cow

My old _____ is _____.

Dictation ···

_____

Listen for It

Day 1 | **Week 25**

Focus: The letter pairs **oi** and **oy** both have the vowel sound you hear in **boy**.

p**oi**nt   j**oy**

Say the picture name. Then read the word.
Underline the letters that stand for the /oi/ sound.

1. oil
2. toy
3. boy
4. boil
5. Roy
6. coin
7. cowboy
8. soil
9. coil

Dictation

1. _____   2. _____   3. _____

Write It

Day 2 | Week 25

Word Box

boy	coin	cowboy
point	oil	toys
soil	coil	boil

Say the picture name. Write the word on the line.
Then circle the letters that have the /oi/ sound.

1.  _____
2.  _____
3. _____

4.  _____
5.  _____
6. _____

7. 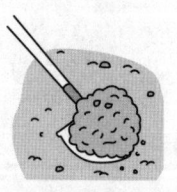 _____
8.  _____
9. _____

Dictation

1. _____   2. _____   3. _____

Write It

Day 3 | Week 25

Word Box

enjoy	boy	point
boil	coil	Roy
cowboy	noise	toy

Read each word in the Word Box. Write the word under the correct letters.

oi	oy
_____	_____
_____	_____
_____	_____
_____	_____

Dictation

_____

Read It

Day 4 | Week 25

Read the words. Underline the letters that stand for the **/oi/** sound. Then draw a line to the correct picture.

1. **toy** mouse

2. **boil** and bubble

3. jump for **joy**

4. happy **cowboy**

5. old **coin**

6. bottle of **oil**

Dictation

Read It

Day 5 | Week 25

Write the missing words. Then read the sentence.

1. boy   Roy

   _____ is a nice _____.

2. cowboy   coin

   The _____ has a _____.

3. noise   toy

   The _____ makes a lot of _____.

4. soil   oil

   Do not put _____ in the _____!

Dictation

Listen for It

Day 1 | Week 26

Focus: The vowel pair **oo** can have the sound you hear in **wood**. It can also have the sound you hear in **pool**.

w**oo**d   p**oo**l

Say the picture name. Listen to the vowel sound. Then name each picture in the row. Fill in the circle if it has the same vowel sound as the first picture.

1.
2.
3.
4.

Dictation

1. _____   2. _____   3. _____

Write It

Day 2 | Week 26

Word Box

boot	tools	broom
wood	moon	pool
hook	book	tooth

Say the picture name. Write the word on the line.

1.  _____
2.  _____
3.  _____
4.  _____
5.  _____
6. 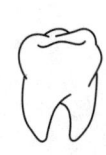 _____
7.  _____
8.  _____
9. _____

Dictation

1. _____   2. _____   3. _____

Write It

Day 3 | Week 26

Word Box

hook	tools	moon
foot	book	room
tooth	shook	boot

Read each word in the Word Box. Write the word under the picture name with the same vowel sound.

w**oo**d

br**oo**m

Dictation

1. _____ 2. _____ 3. _____

Read It

Day 4 | Week 26

Read the words. Underline the letters that stand for the vowel sound in **broom**. Circle the letters that stand for the vowel sound in **wood**. Then draw a line to the matching picture.

1. big **goose**

2. **good book**

3. yellow **moon**

4. brown **boots**

5. deep **pool**

6. one **tooth**

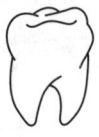

Dictation

1. _____   2. _____   3. _____

Read It

Day 5 | Week 26

Write the missing words. Then read the sentence.

1. zoo   book

   I will read a _____ about a _____.

2. moon   look

   I _____ up at the _____.

3. roof   boot

   There is a _____ on the _____!

4. noon   school

   _____ starts at _____ today.

Dictation

Read It

Day 1 | Week 27

Focus: Sometimes a consonant is **silent**. It does not have a sound. The letter **k** is often silent before **n**. The letter **w** is often **silent** before **r**.

knot

write

Say the picture name. Listen to the letter-sounds.
Cross out the **silent** letter at the beginning of each word.

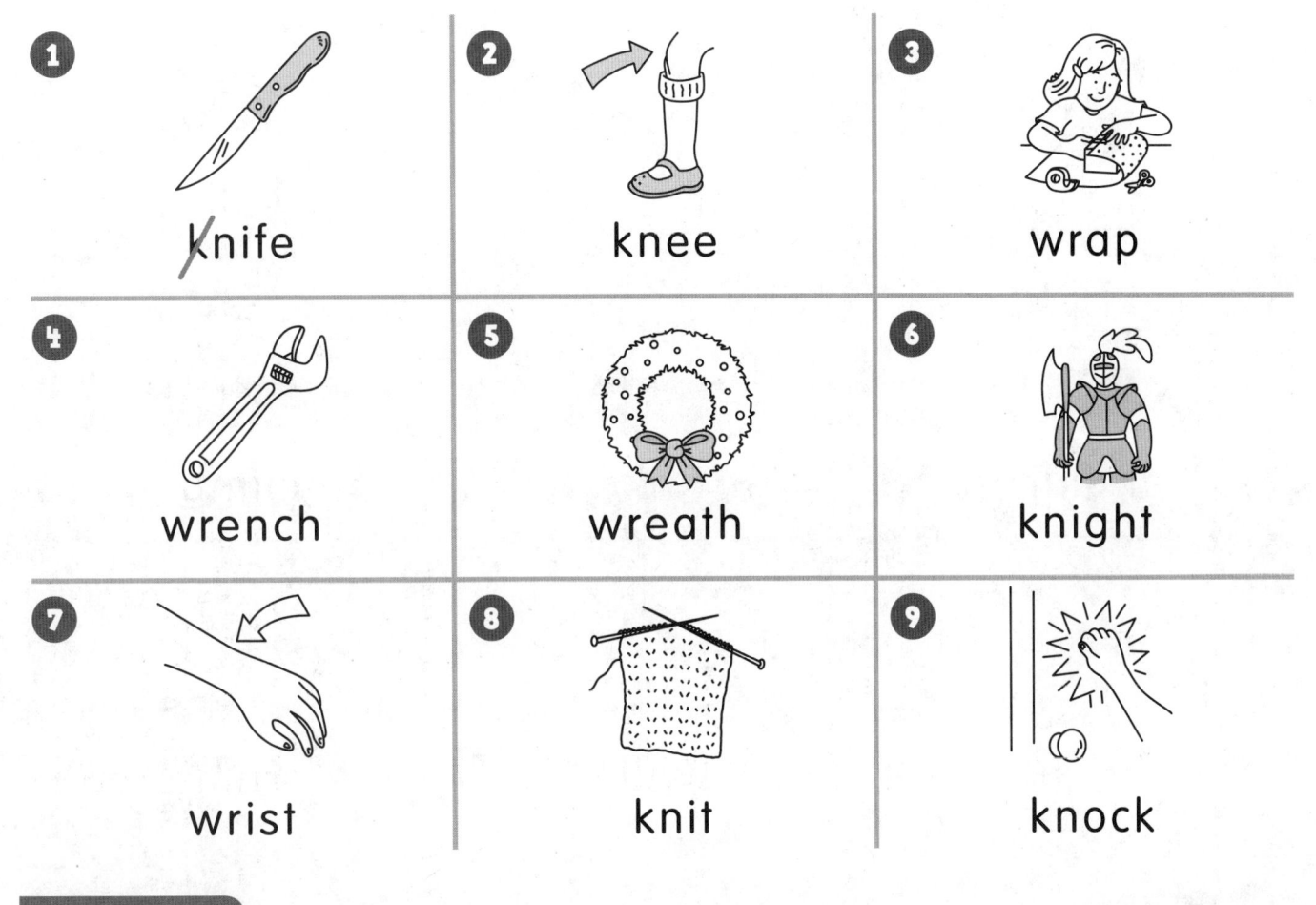

1. ~~k~~nife
2. knee
3. wrap
4. wrench
5. wreath
6. knight
7. wrist
8. knit
9. knock

Dictation

1. _____   2. _____

© Evan-Moor Corp. • EMC 6772 • Daily Phonics

Listen for It

Day 2 | Week 27

Focus: The letter **l** is often silent before the letters **f** and **k**. The letter **b** is silent at the end of some words.

calf | comb

Say the picture name. Listen to the letter-sounds. Cross out the **silent** letter in the word.

1.  lamb
2.  half
3.  yolk
4.  thumb
5.  talk
6.  climb
7. 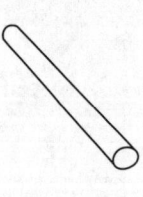 chalk
8.  walk
9.  crumb

Dictation

1. _____   2. _____

132   Daily Phonics • EMC 6772 • © Evan-Moor Corp.

Write It

Day 3 | Week 27

Word Box

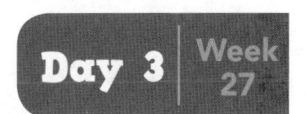

lamb	knife	talk	wrap
knock	chalk	write	climb
calf	crumb	knee	wrist

Read each word in the Word Box. Write the word under the correct silent letter.

silent k
_____
_____
_____

silent w
_____
_____
_____

silent l
_____
_____
_____

silent b
_____
_____
_____

Dictation

_____

Read It

Day 4 | Week 27

Read the words. Underline the **silent** letter in the bold word.
Then draw a line to the matching picture.

1 a tight **knot**

2 a little **crumb**

3 **talk** a lot

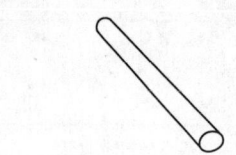

4 white **chalk**

5 an egg **yolk**

6 a sharp **knife**

Dictation

1. _____   2. _____

Read It

Day 5 | Week 27

Write the missing words. Then read the sentence.

1

chalk   write

You can _____ with _____.

2

lamb   comb

You can _____ the _____.

3

yolk   knife

Cut the egg _____ with a _____.

4

climb   knot

Hold onto the _____ and _____ up the rope.

Dictation

Read It

Day 1 | Week 28

Focus: Add an **s** to the end of a word to show more than one. The **s** makes the word **plural**.

cat + **s** = cats

Look at the picture. Fill in the circle next to the correct word.

1. ○ dog ○ dogs

2. ○ bed ○ beds

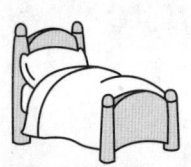

3. ○ car ○ cars

4. ○ webs ○ web

5. ○ hat ○ hats

6. ○ rug ○ rugs

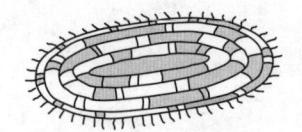

7. ○ kite ○ kites

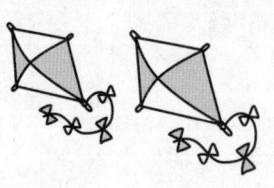

8. ○ bone ○ bones

9. ○ bikes ○ bike

Dictation

1. _____ 2. _____ 3. _____

Write It

Day 2 | Week 28

Focus: Some words have **es** added at the end to make them plural. An **es** is added to words that end in **ss**, **ch**, or **x**.

kiss**es**   bench**es**   box**es**

Look at the picture. Read the word. Write the **plural** form of the word on the line.

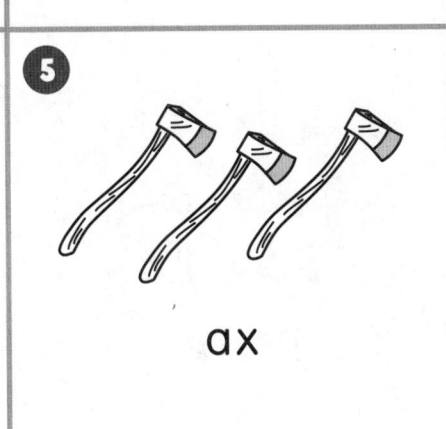

1. dress
   _____

2. fox
   _____

3. peach
   _____

4. glass
   _____

5. ax
   _____

6. lunch
   _____

Dictation ....

_____

© Evan-Moor Corp. • EMC 6772 • Daily Phonics   137

Write It

Day 3 | Week 28

Focus: When a word ends in a consonant and a **y**, change the **y** to **i** and add **es** to make it plural.

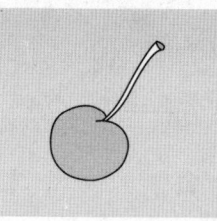

cherr~~y~~ⁱ + **es** = cherries

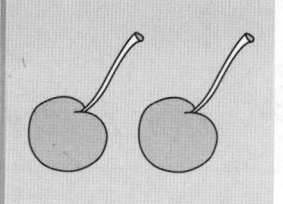

Read the word. Cross out the **y** and write the word with **ies** to make it plural.

1  pony _____

2  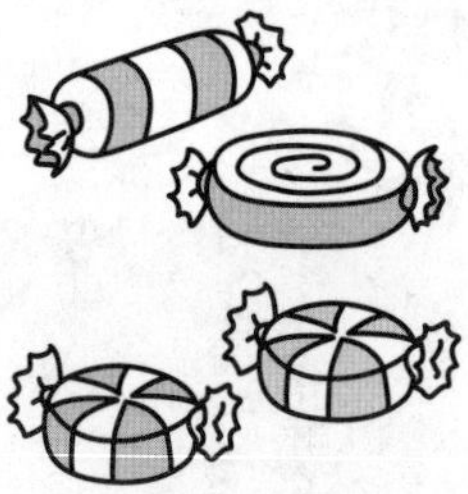 candy _____

3  berry _____

4  daisy _____

5  puppy _____

6  penny _____

Dictation

1. part _____   2. stor _____   3. famil _____

Write It

Day 4 | Week 28

Follow the rule to make the word **plural**.
Write the plural form on the line.

add **s**	add **es**	change the **y** to **i** and add **es**
bed __beds__	pass __passes__	family __families__
cup _____	fox _____	party _____
dog _____	glass _____	cherry _____
girl _____	peach _____	pony _____
bone _____	bench _____	candy _____
cake _____	dress _____	berry _____

Dictation

1. kite _____   2. gas _____   3. lad _____

Read It

Day 5 | Week 28

Write the missing words. Then read the sentence.

1. dresses   ladies

The _____ wore _____.

2. parties   cakes

We made _____ for two _____.

3. bones   dogs

The _____ have _____.

4. books   glasses

I put on my _____ to read _____.

Dictation

Listen for It

Day 1 | **Week 29**

Focus: Some words change spellings when they change from singular to plural.

singular
man

plural
men

Say the picture name. Read the word.
Then draw a line to match the word to its plural form.

1. mouse • • women
2. foot • • teeth
3. woman • • mice
4. tooth • • leaves
5. goose • • feet
6. leaf • • geese

Dictation

1. tooth _____   2. leaf _____

© Evan-Moor Corp. • EMC 6772 • Daily Phonics

Write It

Day 2 | Week 29

Word Box

goose	teeth	mouse	foot
feet	lives	women	life
tooth	woman	mice	geese

Read each word in the Word Box. Write the singular form under **one**. Then write the plural form under **more than one**.

singular **one**	plural **more than one**
_____	_____
_____	_____
_____	_____
_____	_____
_____	_____

Dictation

_____

Write It

Day 3 | Week 29

Word Box

teeth   geese   women
hooves children mice

Complete the phrase by writing the plural form of the underlined word.

1.  one mouse, three _____

2. 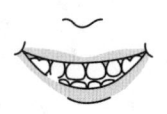 a tooth, many _____

3.  one goose, two _____

4.  a woman, many _____

5.  a child, six _____

6.  one hoof, two _____

Dictation

1. man _____   2. life _____

Read It

Day 4 | Week 29

Read the incomplete sentence. Write the correct word on the line.
Then read the sentence again.

1. I have a loose _____.
   tooth   teeth

2. All of the _____ want candy.
   child   children

3. One _____ walked by me.
   goose   geese

4. I saw three _____ today.
   mouse   mice

5. I have two _____.
   foot   feet

6. Five _____ rode their bikes.
   man   men

Dictation ···

1. hoof _____   2. woman _____

Read It

Day 5 | Week 29

Word Box

woman   geese   mouse
teeth   men   feet

Write the missing words to complete the sentence. Then read the sentence.

1.  The _____ sees a _____.

2.  _____ do not have _____.

3.  The _____ have big _____.

Dictation ....

Write It

Day 1 | Week 30

Focus: When a verb ends with **ed**, it means that the action already happened. When a verb ends with **ing**, it means that the action is or was in the process of happening.

action	+ ed	+ ing
I jump.	I jump**ed**.	I am jump**ing**. I was jump**ing**.

Read the words. Circle **ed** and **ing**. Then write the base word on the line.

+ ed	+ ing	action (base word)
1. turn**ed**	turn**ing**	turn
2. stamped	stamping	_____
3. parked	parking	_____
4. started	starting	_____
5. melted	melting	_____
6. helped	helping	_____
7. looked	looking	_____

Dictation

1. _____   2. _____   3. _____

Write It

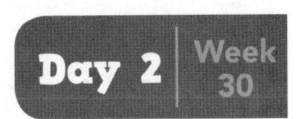

Day 2 | Week 30

Focus: When a verb ends with a consonant and a silent **e**, the silent **e** is dropped before **ed** or **ing** is added.

action	+ ed	+ ing
I bake.	I bak**ed**.	I am bak**ing**. I was bak**ing**.

Read the words. Circle **ed** and **ing**. Then write the base word on the line.

+ ed	+ ing	action (base word)
1. tap(ed)	tap(ing)	tape
2. hiked	hiking	_____
3. saved	saving	_____
4. tasted	tasting	_____
5. raked	raking	_____
6. voted	voting	_____
7. moved	moving	_____

Dictation

1. _____   2. _____   3. _____

Write It

Day 3 | Week 30

Focus: When a verb ends with one short vowel and one consonant, the final consonant is doubled before **ing** or **ed** is added.

action	+ **ed**	+ **ing**
hop	hop**ped**	hop**ping**

Read the word. Then write the word and follow the rule to add **ed**.
Write the word again and follow the rule to add **ing**.

action (base word)	+ **ed**	+ **ing**
1. trip	tripped	tripping
2. stop		
3. tap		
4. brag		
5. skip		
6. shop		
7. wrap		

Dictation ··

1. _____   2. _____   3. _____

Write It

Day 4 | Week 30

Follow the rule to change the verb forms. Write the words on the lines.

Add **ed** to show that the action already happened.
Add **ing** to show that the action is or was happening.

action	+ ed	+ ing
1. kick	_____	_____
2. talk	_____	_____
3. start	_____	_____

Cross out the silent **e** before adding **ed** or **ing**.

action	+ ed	+ ing
4. trade	_____	_____
5. shine	_____	_____
6. smile	_____	_____

Double the consonant before adding **ed** or **ing**.

action	+ ed	+ ing
7. rip	_____	_____
8. nap	_____	_____
9. drag	_____	_____

Dictation

1. _____   2. _____   3. _____

Read It

Day 5 | Week 30

Read the incomplete sentence. Write the correct word on the line. Then read the sentence again.

1. The boys _____ ball last night.
   playing   played

2. We went _____ and used our tent.
   camping   camped

3. I am _____ the leaves in the yard.
   raking   raked

4. The dog _____ the ball.
   chasing   chased

5. The rabbit _____ across the grass.
   hopping   hopped

6. My sister was _____ to the music.
   skipping   skipped

Dictation ··

Read It

Day 1 | Week 31

Focus: A **prefix** is a word part added to the **beginning** of a word. A **prefix** changes the meaning of the word.

dis = not   **re** = again   **un** = not or the opposite of

un + kind = **un**kind

Read the word and its meaning. Underline the prefix.

1 **rewrite** to write again	2 **undone** the opposite of **done**	3 **disarm** to make not armed
4 **unhappy** not happy	5 **reheat** to heat again	6 **disable** to make not able to work
7 **dislike** to not like	8 **return** to go back again	9 **unsure** not sure

Dictation

1. _____   2. _____   3. _____

Write It

Day 2 | Week 31

Word Box

dislike	unwrap	rewrite	unhappy
rewrap	discover	refold	disappear
unkind	disagree	reheat	undress

Read each word in the Word Box. Write the word under the correct prefix. Then underline the base word.

dis- not	**re-** again	**un-** not/opposite of
_____	_____	_____
_____	_____	_____
_____	_____	_____
_____	_____	_____

Dictation ··

_____

Read It

Day 3 | Week 31

Draw a line to match the word to its meaning.

1. distrust • not happy

2. repaint • to not like

3. unhappy • to not trust someone

4. dislike • not able to do something

5. return • to paint again

6. unable • to go back again

7. disagree • to fold something again

8. refold • not nice to other people

9. unkind • to have a different idea than someone else

Dictation

1. _____ 2. _____ 3. _____

Write It

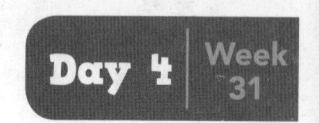

Day 4 | Week 31

Prefix Box

dis   re   un

Read the incomplete sentence.
Write the correct prefix to complete the sentence.

1 I _____like going to bed early.

2 They had to _____paint the house.

3 May I _____wrap my gift now?

4 When will Marcus _____turn home?

5 I _____trust people who lie.

6 I felt _____happy when my friend left.

Dictation ···

Read It

Day 5 | Week 31

Read the incomplete sentence. Write the correct word on the line. Then read the sentence again.

1. Sara had to _____ the gift.
   rewrap   rewrite

2. I am _____ to go to the party.
   disable   unable

3. The police officer had to _____ the robber.
   disarm   rearm

4. Please _____ before you go to bed.
   undress   disdress

5. Dad will _____ the gate.
   rewrap   repaint

6. Did the snake _____ down the hole?
   disappear   disagree

Dictation ....

Read It

Day 1 | Week 32

Focus: A **suffix** is a word part added to the **end** of a word. A **suffix** changes the meaning of the word.

ful = full of   **less** = without   **ly** = in a certain way

help + **ful** = helpful

Read the word. Underline the suffix.

1 harmless	2 hopeful	3 kindly
4 useful	5 restless	6 softly
7 quickly	8 wonderful	9 helpless
10 fearless	11 sadly	12 joyful

Dictation

1. _____   2. _____   3. _____

Write It

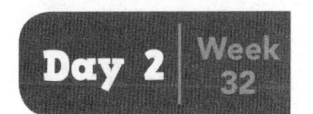

Day 2 | Week 32

Word Box

joyful	sadly	pointless	careless
fearless	hopeful	softly	useful
quickly	dreadful	harmless	loudly

Read each word in the Word Box. Write the word under the correct suffix. Then underline the base word.

-ful full of	**-less** without	**-ly** in a certain way
_____	_____	_____
_____	_____	_____
_____	_____	_____
_____	_____	_____

Dictation

_____

Read It

Day 3 | Week 32

Draw a line to match the word to its meaning.

1. joyful • in a fast way

2. fearless • a help to others

3. quickly • without fear

4. harmless • very happy

5. helpful • in a sad way

6. sadly • without harm

7. pointless • without purpose

8. softly • a help to someone

9. useful • in a quiet way; in a gentle way

Dictation

1. _____ 2. _____ 3. _____

Write It

Suffix Box

ful   less   ly

Read the incomplete sentence.
Write the correct suffix to complete the sentence.

1. The kind_____ woman gave me a cookie.

2. My sister is not very help_____ when we bake.

3. How quick_____ can you run home?

4. It was point_____ to try to fix the broken glass.

5. The popped balloon was use_____.

6. Be care_____ when you cross the street.

Dictation

Read It

Day 5 | Week 32

Read the incomplete sentence. Write the correct word on the line. Then read the sentence again.

1. A garden snake is _____ to people.
   harmless   restless

2. The dancer was very _____.
   graceful   quickly

3. A tiny kitten is _____.
   helpful   helpless

4. The brave firefighter was _____.
   fearful   fearless

5. Be _____ when you use a knife.
   careful   careless

6. Henry whispered _____ to his sister.
   softly   hopeful

Dictation ···